Welfare Reform in California

Early Results from the Impact Analysis

Jacob Alex Klerman

V. Joseph Hotz

Elaine Reardon

Amy G. Cox

Donna O. Farley

Steven J. Haider

Guido Imbens

Robert Schoeni

MR-1358-CDSS

Prepared for the California Department of Social Services

LABOR AND POPULATION

The research described in this report was prepared for the California Department of Social Services under Contract No. H38030.

Library of Congress Cataloging-in-Publication Data

Welfare reform in California : early results from the impact analysis / Jacob A. Klerman ... [et al.].
    p. cm.
    "MR-1358."
    Includes bibliographical references.
    ISBN 0-8330-3039-6
    1. Welfare recipients—Employment—California. 2. California Work Opportunity and Responsibility to Kids (Program) 3. Public welfare—California. I. Klerman, Jacob Alex.

HV98.C3 W43 2001
362.5'8'09794—dc21

                                                                2001041901

RAND is a nonprofit institution that helps improve policy and decisionmaking through research and analysis. RAND® is a registered trademark. RAND's publications do not necessarily reflect the opinions or policies of its research sponsors.

Published 2003 by RAND
1700 Main Street, P.O. Box 2138, Santa Monica, CA 90407-2138
1200 South Hayes Street, Arlington, VA 22202-5050
201 North Craig Street, Suite 202, Pittsburgh, PA 15213
RAND URL: http://www.rand.org/
To order RAND documents or to obtain additional information, contact Distribution Services: Telephone: (310) 451-7002; Fax: (310) 451-6915; Email: order@rand.org

Preface

In response to national welfare reform legislation, California passed legislation on August 11, 1997, that replaced the existing Aid to Families with Dependent Children (AFDC) and Greater Avenues for Independence (GAIN) programs with the California Work Opportunity and Responsibility to Kids (CalWORKs) program. Following an open and competitive bidding process, the California Department of Social Services (CDSS), which administers CalWORKs, awarded a contract to RAND to conduct a statewide evaluation of the CalWORKs program.

This RAND report presents early results on the impact of the CalWORKs program. In particular, it presents analyses of national data (administrative data on caseloads and national survey data on household income) and statewide data (on caseloads, employment, and earnings). An executive summary of this report is published separately in *Welfare Reform in California: Early Results from the Impact Analysis, Executive Summary* (MR-1358/1-CDSS).

This is the first of two reports on the impact of CalWORKs. The second impact analysis report will appear in mid-2002.

The implementation of the CalWORKs program is described in a parallel set of process analysis reports. The second of these, *Welfare Reform in California: State and County Implementation of CalWORKs in the Second Year* (MR-1177-CDSS) and its corresponding executive summary, *Welfare Reform in California: State and County Implementation of CalWORKs in the Second Year* (MR-1177/1-CDSS), were released in February 2001.

For more information about the evaluation, see **http://www.rand.org/CalWORKs** or contact:

Jacob Alex Klerman
RAND
1700 Main Street
P.O. Box 2138
Santa Monica, CA 90407-2138
(310) 393-0411 x6289
klerman@rand.org

Aris St. James
CDSS
744 P Street, MS 12-56
Sacramento, CA 95814
(916) 657-1959
astjames@dss.ca.gov

Contents

Figures

Tables

Summary

Background

In response to federal welfare reform—the Personal Responsibility and Work Opportunity Reconciliation Act of 1996 (PRWORA)—California enacted the Thompson-Maddy-Ducheny-Ashburn Welfare-to-Work Act of 1997 on August 11, 1997. That legislation replaced the Aid to Families with Dependent Children (AFDC) program and Greater Avenues for Independence (GAIN), the state's associated welfare-to-work (WTW) program, with the California Work Opportunity and Responsibility to Kids (CalWORKs) program.

CalWORKs is a modified "work-first" program that provides services to help welfare recipients move from welfare to work and toward self-sufficiency. Most recipients have Job Club (a structured job search program) as their first activity, although some go directly to assessment and other activities to improve their job readiness. CalWORKs also imposes lifetime limits on the receipt of cash assistance by adults to further motivate recipients to make these transitions. Finally, CalWORKs devolves to California's 58 counties increased flexibility and financial accountability in designing their welfare programs. With the enactment of the CalWORKs legislation, the California Department of Social Services (CDSS) and the county welfare departments (CWDs) moved promptly to design and implement the new programs, a process that lasted well into calendar year 1999.[1]

Objectives and Approach

This report, prepared by RAND under contract from CDSS as part of the Statewide CalWORKs Evaluation, is the first of two reports on the impact of CalWORKs. The report's structure and analyses are guided by a conceptual model of the pathways through which welfare reform and other factors affect work activity participation rates, welfare caseloads, and outcomes for welfare leavers. These outcomes, as well as the ways they vary through time, between California and the other states, and across California's 58 counties, are affected

---

[1]See Klerman et al., 2001.

by multiple factors. The effects of some of these factors—"policy effects"—flow directly from changes to California statute; the effects of other factors—"program effects"—flow indirectly through policy and funding of the 58 CWDs that provide eligibility operations and WTW services to individual welfare recipients.

The CalWORKs reforms were not the only factors affecting outcomes. These reforms built on earlier reforms in California, in particular, changes to the structure of benefits as part of the 1993 Work Pays Demonstration Project and a more work-first-focused WTW program as part of the 1995 reform of GAIN. Other government policies also affected outcomes, in particular, massive increases in the Earned Income Tax Credit (EITC), federal immigration reform, and increases in California's minimum wage. Finally, CalWORKs was implemented during a period of strong economic expansion. All of these factors would have been expected to affect the outcomes considered here.

This report describes outcomes under CalWORKs through approximately the summer of 2000 and begins the process of explaining the observed variation in outcomes through time, between California and other states, and among California's counties.

Work Activities

PRWORA mandates that increasing fractions of recipients participate in work or a defined set of work activities for a specified number of hours per month. County WTW programs have the dual goals of helping the state achieve those federal statutory goals and helping recipients develop job search skills, work skills, and work experience that will enable them to achieve self-sufficiency and leave cash assistance.

Significant progress has been made in involving recipients in activities. Even though program start-up was slower than anticipated, and despite the exit of the most employable recipients, work participation rates have risen rapidly between federal fiscal year (FFY) 1997 and FFY 1999, and California's participation rates are higher than the national average. Finally, most of California's participants are working, the ideal form of participation, to which nonwork activities are intended to lead.

Despite these relative comparisons, the absolute level of participation in work activities remains low. In FFY 1999, only about one-third of California's one-parent families were participating in a countable activity for the federally required number of hours in a given month (25 hours per week, 20 for those with a child under six years of age). Applying the CalWORKs statute's higher hours requirements (32 hours per week for all recipients with a child over one year old) implies a still lower figure, about one-fourth.

In addition, California's participation rate appears to be higher than the national average primarily because California has a higher proportion of two-parent families and because of the structure of benefits. Two-parent families are much more likely to participate, so a higher proportion of two-parent cases raises the all-families rate. California's one-parent-family participation rate is nearly identical to that of the nation as a whole.

California's high benefit levels, combined with the Work Pays reforms as extended by the CalWORKs legislation, imply that a recipient in a family of three can earn up to the equivalent of full-time work at approximately $8.75 per hour and still be income-eligible for cash assistance. Recomputing the participation rate to include only those individuals with earnings low enough to make them eligible in the other states (actually averaging across the implied caseload for each state) would yield a participation rate below that of the nation as a whole.

Finally, as we noted above, most of the observed participation is in the form of work. However, among those not working, only about one in 10 participates, even when the lower federal hours requirement is applied. Thus, counties are having trouble engaging nonworking recipients in activities for enough hours. Some of these recipients are formally noncompliant (slightly more than 10 percent are in sanction; slightly less than 10 percent are in the formal noncompliance process), but for the balance of mandatory participants, the problem appears to be some combination of cases awaiting an initial meeting with a caseworker, cases between activities, and noncompliant cases that have not yet entered the formal noncompliance process.

Caseload

Part of the motivation for federal welfare reform was the rapid increase in the welfare caseload in the late 1980s and early 1990s. That increase was especially large in California, which experienced a deep recession.

California's welfare caseload peaked in March 1995 and has declined rapidly—about 1 percent per month—since then. The decline is broad-based; it includes almost every county and every racial/ethnic group. It is smallest (and only modest) among child-only cases and largest among two-parent families, with one-parent families—the majority of the cases—also exhibiting a sharp decline. About half the decline has resulted from current recipients' more rapid exit from welfare, and about half has resulted from lower entry rates into welfare. Finally, while California's caseload declined 41 percent from its peak in March 1995 to June 2000, this is not as great as the 56 percent decline in the rest of the nation over the same period.

This report begins the process of considering the causes of this observed variation in California over time, among California's counties, and between California and the rest of the nation. Not all the caseload decline results from CalWORKs reforms. Some of it occurred before the passage of PRWORA in August 1996; more of it, before the passage of CalWORKs in August 1997; and about half of the decline before the implementation of county CalWORKs programs (depending on the definition of implementation, somewhere between late 1998 and late 1999). The timing of the changes and more formal analyses suggest a major role for the economy (which was responsible for perhaps half of the caseload decline), although the changed CalWORKs policies (i.e., work requirements and time limits) seem likely to have contributed after the CalWORKs legislation was enacted, as well as in anticipation of that legislation.

Through most of the 1997–1998 period, the effect of the county WTW programs on caseloads was probably small. Those programs did not begin to reach large numbers of recipients until late 1998 at the earliest. Furthermore, they would primarily be expected to affect exits from cash assistance, and, as noted earlier, only about half of the caseload decline resulted from higher exit rates. Finally, the evidence from random-assignment studies of work-first programs (e.g., Riverside GAIN) suggests only a modest effect on the welfare caseload.

The slower caseload decline in California in the earlier period appears to be partly the result of California's deeper and longer recession. The emerging national literature points to other factors in the immediate pre-PRWORA and post-PRWORA periods. The CalWORKs program emphasizes positive inducements to work and leave welfare, e.g., recipients keep half their earnings and receive services from a well-funded and varied WTW program that helps them find jobs. In contrast, under waivers in the immediate pre-PRWORA period and then in their Temporary Assistance for Needy Families (TANF) programs under PRWORA, most other states chose policies that emphasize negative inducements—mandatory pre-application job search, strong individual immediate-participation requirements, full-family sanctions, and short lifetime limits on cash assistance leading to terminating assistance to the entire family. California's choice to emphasize positive inducements probably explains some of its smaller caseload decline.

After Welfare

By itself, the caseload is an ambiguous measure of welfare program success. If the goal was only to cut the caseload, one approach would be to eliminate the program. Instead, the goal appears to be to have recipients leave welfare for work and a better life. Conversely, if recipients were being pushed off welfare too soon, we would expect low levels of employment and earnings, high rates of return to welfare, and high levels of poverty.

In fact, there is little evidence for the negative outcomes predicted by some opponents of welfare reform. Even with the substantial caseload decline, welfare leavers today have higher levels of employment and higher levels of earnings than did those in the pre-CalWORKs period. On average, earnings grow with time off aid. Welfare leavers today are less likely to return to welfare than they were in the past. Finally, both in California and in the rest of the nation, poverty levels for all children and for single mothers have fallen sharply.

Thus, the trends are positive. Outcomes are improving through time. In many cases, however, the levels remain low. About one-third of leavers appear not to be working at all. About half of those who are working appear to be earning less than the equivalent of full-time work at the minimum wage. Some of this apparent nonwork and low earnings may be the result of earnings that are not recorded in the Employment Development Department's (EDD) data on which the results are based. RAND's household survey, the California Health and Social Services Survey (CHSSS)—along with several other analyses currently under way—are exploring this data quality issue.

Some have pointed to these low earnings as evidence of the insufficiency of a work-first approach. They argue that CalWORKs should be reoriented to raise recipients' skills through additional education and training, which would increase their market wages. Some counties have implemented or are exploring program initiatives to encourage recipients to seek additional education and training.

The role of additional education and training should be considered in the context of the full "work support system" in California. For welfare leavers, that work support system includes the federal EITC, Food Stamps, Medi-Cal, child care, and transportation (at county option). In total, the system's cash (the federal EITC) and near-cash (Food Stamps) benefits, when added to full-time earnings at California's recently raised minimum wage ($6.25 per hour as of January 2001), are sufficient to lift a family of three about 25 percent above the federal poverty line. Furthermore, when the value of the in-kind benefits (child care, Medi-Cal, and transportation assistance) provided without cost and tax free (for a year or more after leaving welfare) are included, the package's value exceeds the California Budget Project's estimate of the cost of raising a family in California. Finally, the true package is likely to be even larger. The national evidence and limited evidence for California suggest that average wages of those working while on welfare and welfare leavers are over $7 per hour, and in California a household remains eligible for cash assistance until the equivalent of full-time work at about $8.75 per hour.

Thus, after the CalWORKs reforms, work pays. If leavers worked a full-time job at the minimum wage, they would be out of poverty and above the California Budget Project's estimate of the cost of raising a family in California. The evidence presented here, however, suggests that only about one-fourth of welfare leavers have earnings equivalent to full-time work at the (pre-2001, $5.75 per hour) minimum wage.

Conclusions

This first report on the results of the Statewide CalWORKs Evaluation's impact analysis finds almost uniform improvement in outcomes since the implementation of CalWORKs. While the CalWORKs reforms appear to have been responsible for some of that improvement, the robust economy and other policy changes were probably also important.

The rest of the nation has experienced similar improvements in outcomes. Policy choices (the benefit structure, sanction policy, and time-limit policy) appear to be largely responsible for California's higher participation rate and smaller caseload decline.

Whether the state's smaller caseload decline as a result of these policy choices is a cause for concern is far from clear. Lower benefit levels would imply fewer monetary resources for the state's poorest families. Welfare program choices that would cut the caseload—larger and swifter sanctions and shorter time limits— would also be likely to leave some children worse off.

The policy choices in the CalWORKs legislation are broadly consistent with California's policies in the pre-PRWORA period. Presumably, they reflect the state's balancing of the higher safety net for children against the resulting larger welfare caseload, including its higher cost and greater dependency. If the perception of the appropriate balance has shifted, cutting the welfare benefit, more strictly imposing the universal participation requirement, streamlining the conciliation process, cutting the time limit, and removing the continuing payment to the child(ren) would each probably cut the welfare caseload—at the cost of significantly decreasing the financial resources available to children.

Next Steps

Four tasks remain for the coming year and the second report on the impact of CalWORKs. First, the second report will incorporate another year of experience with the CalWORKs program and with the PRWORA programs in other states, which will help to develop a fuller understanding of the outcomes and the causes of those outcomes and which will also help in conducting a cost/benefit analysis of CalWORKs programs.

Second, over the balance of the project, we will consider a wider range of outcomes. In particular, two separate reports will present results from the first and second waves of the CHSSS survey of current and recent welfare recipients. This survey will collect information on experiences in interacting with CWDs and broader measures of household well-being.

Third, this report has begun the task of understanding the causes of the trends in outcomes for California and differential outcomes for California versus the rest of the nation. Over the next year, we will extend and expand these analyses and also draw on the rapidly expanding national literature on these issues.

Fourth, the second report will turn to understanding the differential effects of the welfare programs in each of California's 58 counties. Those programs have only recently settled down into a post-surge steady state. Furthermore, with more data, we can explore the intermediate-term effects of the programs on caseloads, earnings, and return to welfare. In addition, the analyses in this report consider separately employment and earnings of current welfare recipients and of welfare leavers. In the second report we will also explore employment, earnings, and return to welfare among cohorts of those entering or on welfare, not conditional on exit from, or return to, welfare.

Acknowledgments

Beyond those doing the analysis and writing, a document like this appears only through the sustained efforts of three groups of people: those preparing the data, those providing formal comments and formal reviews, and those responsible for the technical preparation of the manuscripts. We wish to acknowledge the help of all three groups here.

Specifically, we wish to thank the large and talented group of RAND programmers who have worked on various components of this project under the leadership of Jan Hanley. They include Christine DeMartini, Rodger Madison, Laurie MacDonald, Craig Martin, Beth Roth, Debbie Wesley, and Shaoling Zhu. Research assistants on this project include Dionne Barnes, Glenn Daley, Caroline Danielson, Wesley Hartman, Alison Jacknowitz, Oscar Mitnik, Julie Mortimer, Sarah Remes, and Marika Suttorp.

We have been helped in understanding the data at the state level by Aris St. James, Paul Smilanick, Tom Burke, Joeana Carpenter, and at the county level by the current and former County Coordinators in each of the six focus counties: Mark Woo and Jim Cunniff, Alameda County; Denice Dotson, Butte County; Marlene Pascua, Fresno County; Althea Shirley, Los Angeles County; Kathleen Stark and Inslee Pitou, Sacramento County; and Kay Riley and Jolie Ramage, San Diego County. Similarly, current and former senior staff in CDSS and its Research and Evaluation Branch—Eloise Anderson, Rita Saenz, Bruce Wagstaff, Charlee Metsker, Jo Weber, Werner Schink, Lois VanBeers, Nikki Baumrind, Larry Carr, Joeanna Carpenter, Michael Pearson, and Webb Hester—have supported our efforts in ways both direct and indirect and too numerous to mention.

Within RAND, we have benefited from the formal review of David Loughran and the external review of Maria Cancian of the University of Wisconsin, Madison. In addition, this document incorporates the efforts and comments of many other members of the RAND research staff.

Finally, a document such as this emerges because of the dedicated behind-the-scenes efforts of secretaries and publications staff members. They receive the document late and are expected to make up the time in their activities. They have handled the time pressures with grace and charity. Secretaries working on this document include Christopher Dirks, Natasha Kostan, and Patrice Lester.

We are also grateful to Janet DeLand and to the staff of RAND's Publications Department who worked on this document under an impossibly tight schedule. Led by Paul Murphy, they include David Bolhuis, Sandy Petitjean, and Benson Wong.

Acronyms and Abbreviations

AB	Assembly Bill
ACF	Administration for Children and Families
AFDC	Aid to Families with Dependent Children
BRR	benefit reduction rate
CalWORKs	California Work Opportunity and Responsibility to Kids Act of 1997
CDHS	California Department of Health Services
CDSS	California Department of Social Services
CHIP	Child Health Insurance Program
CNI	California Needs Index
COLA	cost-of-living adjustment
CPI-U	Consumer Price Index–Urban Consumers
CPS	Current Population Survey
CS	community service
CWD	County Welfare Department
DHHS	U.S. Department of Health and Human Services
DoL	U.S. Department of Labor
EDD	Employment Development Department
EH	"Edwards Hold"
EITC	Earned Income Tax Credit
FFY	federal fiscal year (October–September)
FLSA	Fair Labor Standards Act (minimum wage law)
FSA	Family Support Act of 1988
FY	fiscal year
GAIN	Greater Avenues for Independence
JOBS	Job Opportunities and Basic Skills (training program)
MDRC	Manpower Demonstration Research Corporation
MEDS	Medi-Cal Eligibility Data System
MOE	Maintenance of Effort (requirement)
OJT	On-the-job training
PRWORA	Personal Responsibility and Work Opportunity Reconciliation Act of 1996
SFY	state fiscal year (July–June)
SSI	Supplemental Security Income

SSP	Separate State Program
TANF	Temporary Assistance for Needy Families
UI	Unemployment Insurance
USDA	U.S. Department of Agriculture
Work Pays	California's Assistance Payments and Work Pays Demonstration Project
WtW	U.S. Department of Labor Welfare-to-Work grants
WTW	welfare-to-work

1. Introduction

Background

In response to federal welfare reform—the Personal Responsibility and Work Opportunity Reconciliation Act of 1996 (PRWORA)—California enacted the Thompson-Maddy-Ducheny-Ashburn Welfare-to-Work Act of 1997 on August 11, 1997. That legislation replaced the Aid to Families with Dependent Children (AFDC) program and Greater Avenues for Independence (GAIN), the state's associated welfare-to-work (WTW) program, with the California Work Opportunity and Responsibility to Kids (CalWORKs) program.

CalWORKs is a modified "work-first" program that provides support services to help recipients move from welfare to work and toward self-sufficiency. Beyond encouraging these transitions, CalWORKs also imposes lifetime limits on the receipt of cash assistance by adults. Finally, CalWORKs devolves to California's 58 counties increased flexibility and financial accountability in designing their welfare programs. With the enactment of the legislation, the California Department of Social Services (CDSS)—the state agency responsible for welfare—and the county welfare departments (CWDs) moved promptly to design and implement the new programs, a process that lasted well into calendar year 1999.[1]

The CalWORKs legislation required an independent, comprehensive statewide evaluation of the CalWORKs program. CDSS contracted with RAND for an independent evaluation that would assess both the process of implementing CalWORKs by CDSS, the counties, and allied agencies and the impact (or outcomes) of that implementation on recipients, at both the state and county levels.[2] Two of three process analysis reports have already appeared[3]; this is the first of two impact analysis reports.[4]

---

[1]See Klerman et al., 2001.

[2]For an overview of the evaluation, see Klerman, Reardon, and Steinberg, 1998.

[3]The first process analysis report series included Zellman et al., 1999a,b; and Ebener and Klerman, 1999. The second process analysis report series included Klerman et al., 2001; Klerman, Zellman, and Steinberg, 2001; Ebener and Klerman, 2001; and Cox, Humphrey, and Klerman, 2001. See http://www.rand.org/CalWORKs.

[4]Plans for the impact analysis are described in Klerman et al., 2000; and Haider et al., 2000.

Objectives and Conceptual Model

While the process analysis tries to describe what the welfare agencies did, the impact analysis tries to describe outcomes—the experiences of recipients. In particular, the impact analysis has three objectives: (1) to describe outcomes under CalWORKs and compare them across time, across states, and among California's counties; (2) to identify, as much as possible, the net effect of CalWORKs, given all the other causal factors; and (3) to conduct a cost/benefit assessment of the CalWORKs program.

To help guide our efforts, we developed a simple model illustrating how we conceptualize the impact analysis. We want to describe outcomes under CalWORKs (the topmost white box in Figure 1.1). While there are a number of outcomes of interest, we focus on the three shown in the box (participation rates, employment, and earnings of current recipients; the size and composition of the welfare caseload; and return to welfare, employment, earnings, poverty, and Medi-Cal coverage).

This task of description extends beyond current outcomes in California as a whole, as shown by the additional boxes behind the white outcomes box in the

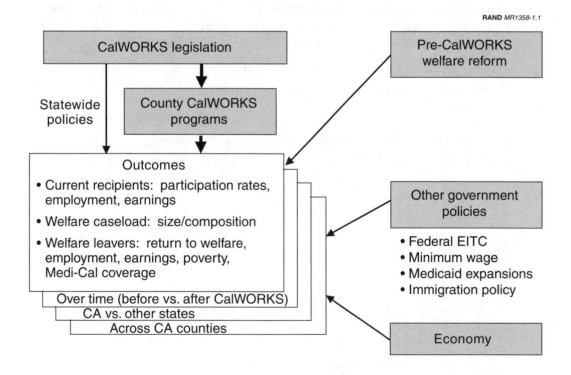

Figure 1.1—Simple Model of How We View the Impact Analysis

figure. Specifically, we describe changes over time (i.e., before and after CalWORKs), differences between California and the other states, and differences across California's 58 counties.

Beyond describing outcomes and how they differ across time and place, we want to understand why they differ. The shaded boxes in Figure 1.1 represent some of the reasons why outcomes might differ. Our primary interest in this evaluation is the assessment of the effect of the CalWORKs legislation, which affects outcomes both directly ("Statewide policies" in the figure) and indirectly— through its effects on CWDs and the welfare programs they implement in their ongoing relations with recipients ("County CalWORKs programs").[5] In addition, non-CalWORKs factors (the shaded boxes on the right) also affect outcomes. Those factors include pre-CalWORKs welfare reforms, other government policies, and the economy. We provide a brief review of each of these factors, starting with the pre-CalWORKs welfare reforms.[6]

Pre-CalWORKs Welfare Reforms

Improvement in outcomes before or shortly after CalWORKs may be the result of pre-CalWORKs welfare reforms. In some cases, those reforms anticipate federal welfare reforms and the details of CalWORKs. Among the recent pre-CalWORKs changes to California's welfare policies are the following:

- *Cuts in the benefit level*: During California's financial crisis in the early 1990s, the cost-of-living adjustment (COLA) was suspended and the benefit was cut several times. In real terms, the cumulative effect was a cut in the real benefit of about 30 percent between 1991 and 1998.

- *Work Pays*: In the early 1990s, a series of changes to the benefit structure encouraged work. In 1992, California adopted fill-the-gap budgeting. Then, starting in September 1993, under a federal waiver, the Work Pays Demonstration Project allowed California welfare recipients to keep more of their earnings (see Appendix A for details). In particular, Work Pays

---

[5]The distinction between "programs" and "policies" is not perfect. Almost all policies require programs to implement them. Without caseworkers and other CWD staff, recipients would not be approved for aid and would not receive monthly checks. The effect of changes to the benefit structure are likely to be larger when caseworkers explain them (Meyers, Glaser, and MacDonald, 1998). Nevertheless, benefit structure can usefully be viewed as primarily a policy set at the state level that directly affects the primary outcomes.

In contrast, the CalWORKs legislation provides only an outline of the WTW services to be provided. From that outline, each CWD developed its own complete program model and provided staff to implement it. In the case of such WTW programs, it is useful to think of the CalWORKs legislation and CDSS activities as only indirectly affecting the primary outcomes.

[6]Appendix A presents a more detailed discussion of these other causal factors and their timing.

4

lowered the benefit reduction rate (BRR). Under prior regulations, recipients kept the first $30 (plus a $90 work allowance) and one-third of earnings above that level (the "thirty and a third" rule), but the former for only a year, and the latter for only four months. The Work Pays reforms extended the time frame for the "thirty and a third" rule indefinitely.

- *AB 1371*: Responding to the findings of the 1994 Manpower Demonstration Research Corporation (MDRC) GAIN Evaluation (Riccio et al., 1994) and the evaluated success of Riverside County's work-first (Job Club-centered) program, the 1995 legislation reoriented the GAIN program from a primarily education-and-training-oriented approach to a more work-first approach. Note, however, that on the eve of CalWORKs reforms, these AB 1371 reforms appear to have been only partially implemented at the county level.

The CalWORKs Reforms

Using the distinction provided earlier, we consider separately the direct effects of the CalWORKs legislation (statewide policies) and the indirect effects (county CalWORKs programs).

The CalWORKs Legislation. Some CalWORKs reforms could have an effect immediately, with only minimal interaction between a recipient and a caseworker or other service provider. This can occur simply with the announcement of the reforms, because people may change their behavior in anticipation of a new policy regime. We refer to the effects of these CalWORKs changes as *legislative effects* or *policy effects*. They include the following:

- *Lifetime time limits*: PRWORA required states to limit lifetime receipt of federally funded assistance by adults to no more than five years. However, in California, unlike in most other states, once this limit is reached, only the portion of the payment for the adult(s) ends; the child(ren)'s portion of the grant will continue as long as the other eligibility criteria are satisfied (e.g., minor children, household income level). Furthermore, California's time-limit clock did not start to tick until January 1998. Thus, the first recipients will not reach time limits until January 2003, which is among the latest dates for any state.[7]

---

[7]The federal time-limit clock started to tick earlier, in December 1996, so recipients will reach lifetime time limits as early as December 2001. However, consistent with delayed implementation of new programs, the CalWORKs legislation delayed the start of state time-limit clocks until January 1998. As a result, no one's aid will be terminated until the later date. The state will pay benefits past the federal time limit (but before the state time limit) from state (nonfederal) maintenance-of-effort (MOE) funds.

- *Higher welfare benefits*: The CalWORKs legislation restored the COLA that had been suspended from 1990 to 1997. California continues to have one of the highest benefit levels of any state.

- *Extended Work Pays reforms*: CalWORKs further extended the approach of the earlier Work Pays reforms, lowering the BRR resulting from earnings from 67 percent to 50 percent, and raising the earned income disregard from $30 (plus a $90 work allowance) to $225. The high benefit level and the low BRR result in a benefit structure that strongly encourages work. This combination also implies that earnings must be quite high (about $8.75 per hour at full-time employment) before a recipient is income-ineligible for CalWORKs.

- *Family caps and minor residence rules*: CalWORKs continued a waiver provision first granted in February 1996 that stated that the welfare benefit is not increased for children conceived while the mother was receiving aid and also requires that minors live with an adult.[8]

- *Continued GAIN sanction procedures*: While the CalWORKs legislation changed many aspects of California's welfare program, it retained the GAIN sanction policy (the formal conciliation process to ensure notification and due process) and GAIN's adults-only maximum sanction (payments for the children continue). This relative stability contrasts with a movement in many other states toward a weaker conciliation process and a full-family sanction.[9]

These legislative changes could have prompted responses with only minimal interaction between a recipient and a caseworker or other service provider, perhaps prior to the actual implementation of CalWORKs.[10]

County CalWORKs Programs. Other CalWORKs reforms could have an effect only (or primarily) through the interactions of caseworkers and contract staff with individual recipients. This, in turn, could occur only after CWD plans were finalized, necessary new staff and contractors were hired and trained, and

---

[8]Food Stamps and Medi-Cal are provided for the child. This change became effective immediately before CalWORKs, on September 1, 1997 (MPP 44-314).

[9]This discussion considers the policy dimension of sanctioning. There is also an important program dimension. For recipients to be sanctioned, a caseworker (often both a WTW worker and an eligibility worker) must implement the time-consuming sanction process. Klerman et al. (2001) report some reluctance to sanction, on the part of both some senior leadership in CWDs and caseworkers. Thus, it appears that sanctions are often imposed considerably less frequently and considerably less quickly than would be allowed under the CalWORKs statute.

[10]See, however, Meyers, Glaser, and MacDonald (1998), who argue that the early effects of the Work Pays reforms were limited because caseworkers did not inform recipients of the changed benefit structure or did not understand its increased incentives for work.

recipients started to participate in program activities. We refer to the effects of these reforms as *program effects*. They include the following:

- *Job Club*: Reflecting the findings of the GAIN Evaluation in Riverside County, where initial Job Club participation had been shown to raise employment, lower cash assistance, and lower net government costs (Riccio et al., 1994), the CalWORKs legislation mandated near-universal Job Club and the corresponding work-first approach to WTW services. This approach contrasted with the more expensive and apparently less successful human-capital development approach and its emphasis on education and training that had been the focus of the GAIN programs in many counties.

- *Intensive WTW services*: For those who did not find jobs through Job Club, the CalWORKs legislation allowed and provided funding for intensive WTW services, including case management, education and training, and supported work. For those with identified barriers to participation, dedicated mental health and substance-abuse funds were available to provide services. In addition, counties could use WTW funds to provide services to victims of domestic violence.

- *Community service*: The CalWORKs legislation provided for mandatory community service (CS) for those not working the mandated number of hours per week within 18/24 months.[11]

Unlike the policy effects discussed earlier, these program effects could be realized only after caseworkers and contractors began to provide services to recipients. By the first quarter of calendar year 2000, county WTW expenditures had nearly tripled over their levels two years earlier. Given the large caseload decline of approximately 20 percent over this same interval, the increase in per-case expenditures was even larger.

The new county WTW programs did not go into place instantaneously. Both qualitative fieldwork and the data on county WTW expenditures (see Appendix A) suggest that it took time to add staff and contractors and then to process the backlog of existing cases. Expenditures did not begin to increase until CDSS certified county CalWORKs plans in the spring of 1998, and a major part of the initial expenditures went to planning, preparing office space, hiring, and training. Participants did not receive significantly higher levels of WTW services until late 1998 or early 1999. Furthermore, WTW expenditures continued to increase at

---

[11]See Klerman et al. (2001) for a discussion of when this period begins and how months are counted. CS is also required for those living in remote locations or unable to participate in other activities.

least over the next year and a half (through the end of state fiscal year, SFY, 1999–2000).

This progressive roll-out affected the time at which existing recipients and new entrants received services. In most counties, Job Club did not begin in volume until late 1998, and the surge to provide services to the existing caseload continued through the summer of 1999 (the spring in some fast-moving counties, the fall in slower-moving ones). Services later in the sequence of activities—e.g., treatment for mental health and substance-abuse issues, education and training, post-employment services—were not provided in volume until late 1999 or even later. Thus, we would not expect the new, more-intensive WTW services to have had much effect until late 1998 at the earliest (and then it was mostly the effect of notification at orientation that welfare programs were changing), growing in about mid-1999 (as recipients moved through Job Club) and later for post-Job Club activities.

Other Government Policies

Welfare programs are not the only government programs or policies that might have affected outcomes. Other candidate government programs include the following, which were shown as bulleted items in Figure 1.1:

- *Federal EITC*: Operating through the tax code, the federal Earned Income Tax credit (EITC) augments the earnings of low-income families with children. The generosity of the program increased sharply in the early 1990s, so that by 2000 those earning about $10,000 per year could receive a payment of nearly $4,000.[12]

- *Minimum wage*: The federal minimum wage rose to $4.75 in 1997 and $5.15 in 1998, and California increased its minimum wage to $5.00 and $5.75 in the same years.

- *Immigration policy*: The 1986 Immigration Reform and Control Act (IRCA) provided procedures through which many previously undocumented immigrants could become U.S. citizens. One of the requirements for legalization was that such individuals could not receive public assistance until five years after their application. Under IRCA, a large number of previously undocumented immigrants were naturalized in 1987 and 1988

---

[12]On the EITC, see Hotz and Scholz (2000). On the effects of the EITC, see Meyer and Rosenbaum (1999, 2000).

and were thus ineligible to receive public assistance until 1992 (and, as the result of a lawsuit, as late as December 1994).

The Economy

The implementation of welfare reform in the late 1990s was coincident with a long and robust economic expansion. We would, in general, expect that an improving economy would lead to improvement in outcomes, including a falling caseload, rising employment and earnings (among current recipients, former recipients, and all single mothers), and falling poverty rates. The recession in California was deeper and lasted longer than in the rest of the nation, but the recovery has been stronger. We would expect these differences to generate differences in California welfare outcomes relative to the rest of the country.

Similarly, the severity of the recession varied widely across the state. There was only a mild recession in the San Francisco Bay area. The recession was much deeper in Southern California, and the recovery stronger. The recession was deep in the northern part of the state, where the recovery has been weaker. Again, we would expect these intercounty differences in economic conditions to generate intercounty differences in welfare outcomes.

Methods

This report describes the evaluation's early efforts to understand the effects of the CalWORKs reforms and other factors on the outcomes of interest. In particular, it lays a foundation by *describing* outcomes across two of the three dimensions shown in Figure 1.1—the post-CalWORKs period compared with the pre-CalWORKs period and California compared with the rest of the nation. It then presents a preliminary discussion of the *causes* of this observed variation.

To understand the analyses of the effect of CalWORKs and the other factors, a brief methodological overview is useful. The causal effect (or impact) of a factor is defined as the difference between observed outcomes and what outcomes would have been if that factor had followed some other path. For example, given the actual CalWORKs program, other policies, and the actual path of the economy, what would have been the effect of California adopting a full-family sanction, holding all else unchanged?

There are three leading approaches to estimating such causal effects: (1) random assignment; (2) nonexperimental program evaluation; and (3) simulation. Here, we briefly discuss each approach. Further discussion can be found in other evaluation reports (e.g., Klerman et al., 2000) and in the national literature on the evaluation of welfare reform (e.g., Moffitt and Ver Ploeg, 1999).

Random Assignment

Some welfare programs (e.g., the GAIN program and the Work Pays Reforms) were analyzed by randomly assigning otherwise identical recipients to either the new program or the old program. Because no control group (i.e., a group not subject to the CalWORKs reforms) was created, random-assignment evaluation of CalWORKs is not possible.[13] Furthermore, it is not clear that such a random-assignment approach could have been used successfully to evaluate the full effects of the CalWORKs reforms. See the discussion in Klerman et al. (2000) and the references therein.

Nonexperimental Program Evaluation

Nonexperimental program evaluation uses statistical models (regression and its generalizations) to estimate causal effects. In particular, nonexperimental program evaluation compares outcomes from multiple policy environments (usually place-year combinations) to try to isolate the effect of a policy (or program).

Ideally, we would compare two policy environments between which only the policy (or program) of interest differed, while everything else was the same. Random assignment approximates that ideal. In the absence of random assignment (which could not be used for CalWORKs), the multiple factors almost always vary. Single policies are rarely adopted alone; instead, policies are usually adopted as bundles. Economic conditions vary across time and space, as do other factors. Nonexperimental program evaluation, then, proceeds using statistical models to control—as much as possible—for the other changing factors and thereby isolate the effect of the policy of interest.

Clearly, to apply this approach, we need variation in the policy of interest. Since multiple policies (and other factors) nearly always vary across policy environments, we need several policy environments. Finally, standard statistical arguments state that the larger the number of "policy environments," the more precise will be our estimates.

---

[13]However, we do use the results of other relevant random-assignment evaluations of welfare reform to help understand some of the potential causes for the outcomes we see.

This need for variation has important implications for our analysis strategy and the presentation of our results. The comparative advantage of this evaluation is access to the rich administrative data available for California. When there is within-California variation, we can use these California data to explore the effects of that variation on outcomes. We report such analyses of the impact of the economy in this report; the next report will consider the effects of county expenditures and program choices.

However, when there is variation through time but not variation between counties in California (as is true for many of the CalWORKs reforms), it is essentially impossible to apply nonexperimental program evaluation methods to our California data. The changes through time could result from any of the CalWORKs reforms, from changes in the economy, or from other factors. Given this multiplicity of possible explanations, it is not possible to distinguish between the effects of the different factors using California data alone.

Instead, application of nonexperimental program evaluation methods usually proceeds using variation both over time and across states (i.e., data on multiple states through time). A national literature is emerging that examines the effects of welfare reform, the pre-TANF (Temporary Assistance for Needy Families) waivers, and state TANF programs. However, such national analyses do not exploit the California administrative data, so we perform only limited such analyses as part of the Statewide CalWORKs Evaluation. In this report, we survey this emerging literature and discuss its implications for understanding California's experiences. Consistent with the currently limited literature, we generally discuss the likely direction and approximate size of effects, but we do not provide exact magnitudes. Perhaps by the second impact analysis report, the literature will have matured enough to enable us to provide more precise statements of effect.

Simulation

When we can precisely describe the mechanism through which a policy affects an outcome and we have appropriate data, we can approximate the effect of a policy through simulation. Simulation is a powerful approach that exploits our knowledge of California's policies and the detailed administrative data. Simulation, however, is only as effective as our ability to describe and to quantify correctly the mechanisms through which policy affects outcomes. Thus, simulation provides insights about the magnitude of the effect of some mechanisms, but it is silent about other mechanisms.

The simulation approach is most easily understood through example. In Section 3, we explore the effect of California's benefit structure on California's work activities participation rate. The structure of California's benefit schedule implies that a recipient can continue receiving cash assistance even when working enough hours to satisfy the participation requirement. By contrast, in many other states, once a recipient is working enough hours to satisfy the participation requirement, her earnings are high enough to make her income-ineligible for cash assistance.[14] This difference raises California's participation rate. If the benefit level were lower, a working (and therefore participating) recipient would no longer be on cash assistance.

We can approximate the size of the effect by simulation. A simple simulation would recompute the participation rate, dropping anyone with earnings high enough to make them income-ineligible in another state. Averaging over the other 49 states gives us a first estimate of the effect of the benefit structure on the participation rate.

However, a calculation of this type assumes that recipients' behavior does not change in response to the policy. In this case, the benefit structure itself is likely to (and intended to) affect hours worked and earnings. A lower BRR would usually be expected to cause current recipients to work more. A higher BRR would be expected to cause recipients to work less. For some cases (including this example), we augment our simulations with other information to incorporate the magnitude of this behavioral response into our simulated estimate of the effect of the policy change.

Data

In conducting our analyses, we used three types of data: (1) county aggregate filings with CDSS (and equivalent filings by states to the federal government)— CA 237 caseload data, GAIN 25/WTW 25/WTW 25A welfare-to-work activity data, and County Expense Claims; (2) individual-level administrative data— Medi-Cal Eligibility Data System (MEDS) caseload data, MEDS-Economic Development Department (EDD) match data employment and earnings data, and Q5 quality control audit system data; and (3) survey data—the U.S. Bureau of the Census Current Population Survey (CPS). Appendix B and Klerman et al. (2000) provide more complete descriptions.

---

[14]While we recognize that both men and women are welfare recipients, most adult welfare recipients are women, so we use the pronouns *she* and *her*.

Scope of This Report

In summary, we have three challenges: (1) to describe outcomes under CalWORKs and compare them across time, across states, and among California's counties; (2) to identify, as much as possible, the net effect of CalWORKs, given all the other confounding factors; and (3) to conduct a cost/benefit assessment of the CalWORKs program.

As the first of two impact analysis reports, this report lays a foundation for the second and final report. Given that goal, the present report focuses on describing outcomes under CalWORKs and on comparing them with outcomes before CalWORKs and in other states; most comparisons of outcomes among California's counties are deferred until next year's report. In terms of the causal analysis, this report provides some exploratory analyses of the role of the CalWORKs program in explaining observed outcomes—why outcomes in California have evolved as they have over time, and why they have evolved differently than in other states. Again, the discussion of why outcomes are different among counties is reserved for next year's report. This report also surveys relevant national literatures for insights into California's experience, especially relative to that of other states. The evaluation's parallel process analysis reports describe the financial aspects of CalWORKs.

The second impact analysis report will extend these analyses. It will update the descriptive analyses reported here through approximately another year of experience with CalWORKs and will add descriptive analyses of additional outcomes. Also, as mentioned above, it will include a much fuller discussion of the cross-county differences. In addition, it will provide more analyses of the causal effects of CalWORKs. Finally, integrating these fuller analyses with the financial results from the process analysis, the report will consider the costs and benefits of the program.

These two impact analysis reports will be augmented by additional results from RAND's California Health and Social Services Survey (CHSSS).

Organization of the Report

This report is organized around the structure shown earlier in Figure 1.1. We first describe each of the three outcomes shown in the figure—both before and after CalWORKs and between California and the rest of the nation—starting with an overview of those descriptive findings and following with the detailed support for them. Finally, we examine the potential causal explanations for the descriptive results, drawing, as appropriate, from the five factors shown in the figure.

Section 2 considers the participation rates and employment and earnings of current welfare recipients. Section 3 considers the size and composition of the caseload. Section 4 considers employment, earnings, and return to receiving aid among welfare leavers, as well as broader outcome measures: Medi-Cal take-up, poverty, and the living arrangements of children. Finally, Section 5 summarizes the results and discusses plans for the coming year.

This report relegates more technical information to the appendices. Appendix A provides a more detailed description of the major policy and economic changes that might influence the outcomes considered here. Appendix B presents additional detail on some of the methods,[15] and Appendix C presents basic information about the data sources and discusses some key data issues.[16] Appendix D presents the results of the policy simulation conducted on participation rates. Finally, Appendix E provides a county-level breakdown of caseload changes over time.

---

[15]Further detail on the analytic methods can be found in the underlying technical reports. Those technical reports are available on the project website: http://www.rand.org/CalWORKs.

[16]Further discussion of data sources can be found in Klerman et al., 2000, and in Klerman and Haider, 2001.

2. Program Participation

Counties use their CalWORKs funds to provide services that are intended to help recipients find jobs, make them self-sufficient, and enable them to leave cash assistance. The services are also intended to engage enough recipients for the state to meet two goals: aggregate federal participation requirements and the CalWORKs legislation's individual participation-rate requirement.[1]

This section considers the evidence of the counties' success in engaging current recipients of cash assistance in WTW activities. We begin with an overview of the descriptive findings on participation rates and California's creation of a separate state program (SSP) for two-parent families in October 1999. We then present a more detailed discussion of the components of participation. Finally, we examine some possible explanations of what might account for the descriptive findings.

Overview of Descriptive Findings

The first goal—meeting federal participation rates—has been satisfied. Despite some concern in federal fiscal year (FFY) 1997 about the two-parent rate, California has met both the all-families and the two-parent participation-rate requirements every year. As a result, the state has borne no federal penalties and has been subject to a lower maintenance of effort (MOE) requirement (75 percent instead of 80 percent of pre-PRWORA spending). Furthermore, California's participation rates are rising and are higher than those of the nation as a whole. With the establishment of the SSP for two-parent families[2] (and probably even without it), the caseload decline and the resulting caseload reduction credit imply that as long as the requirements and the method of computing them remain unchanged and there is not a major recession, California should have no trouble meeting the adjusted targets. However, because the participation rates are similarly not binding in most other states, there is serious discussion about

---

[1]The CalWORKs statute (11320.3) states: "Except as provided in subdivision (b) or if otherwise exempt, every individual, as a condition of eligibility for aid under this chapter, shall participate in welfare-to-work activities under this article."

[2]The establishment of an SSP is likely to decrease the all-families participation rate. Two-parent families have higher participation rates than one-parent families. Thus, the all-families rate is a weighted average of the two groups. Since California has a high proportion of two-parent cases, pulling them out will leave the one-parent families, who have lower participation rates.

toughening the participation-rate requirements as part of TANF renewal (for FFY 2003, beginning October 2002).

The second goal—near-universal, immediate participation in CalWORKs WTW activities (work as well as other activities) for 32 hours per week—has not been met. High participation rates are known to be difficult to achieve (Hamilton and Scrivener, 1999). Some recipients are statutorily exempt; others are in the formal noncompliance process or are sanctioned; and some are between activities. No one expected literally universal participation, but the reported levels appear to be lower than many anticipated. However, most of the participation appears to be work—the most desired form of participation. Among those not working, participation rates are much lower.

Meeting Federal Participation Rates

To understand how California is meeting federal participation rates, we first discuss the components used to determine the rates. Then, we look at how California has fared in terms of "all-families" participation rates and how it has fared in terms of the more complicated "two-parent" rates. Finally, we examine how California compares with the nation as a whole in terms of participation rates for both all families and two-parent families.

Components Used to Determine Participation Rates

PRWORA imposes penalties on states for failure to meet required work activity participation rates both for all families and for two-parent families.[3] For both groups, these have three components, as shown in Table 2.1. First, PRWORA establishes a nominal percentage of the caseload that must be engaged in a work activity. The required percentage rises from 25 percent in FFY 1997 to 50 percent in FFY 2002.

Second, participation is defined using a minimum number of hours per week. The required number of hours also rises, from 20 hours in FFY 1997, to 25 hours in FFY 1999, and to 30 hours in FFY 2000 and following (45CFR261.31).

Third, the work activity participation rates are compared against an "adjusted target." One of PRWORA's stated goals is to reduce dependency, and declines in the caseload are viewed as a direct indicator of progress toward this goal.

_____

[3]The MOE requirement is reduced from 80 percent to 75 percent for states meeting the participation-rate requirement.

Table 2.1

Federal Work Activity Participation-Rate Requirements

	Federal Fiscal Year					
	1997	1998	1999	2000	2001	2002
All families						
Participation rate (percentage of caseloads)	25	30	35	40	45	50
Hours participated per week	20	20	25	30	30	30
Hours participated, child under 6	20	20	20	20	20	20
Two-parent families						
Participation rate (percentage of caseloads)	75	75	90	90	90	90
Hours primary adult participated	35	35	35	35	35	35
Hours spouse participated	20	20	20	20	20	20

NOTE: The FFY begins on October 1 and ends September 30 of the following year. The requirement for two-parent families is 55 hours per week if they receive federally funded child care.

Consistent with this perspective, PRWORA's caseload reduction credit reduces the participation rate required to avoid federal penalties by the percentage decline in the caseload. Along with several other smaller adjustments, this produces the adjusted target.

How California Has Fared in Meeting All-Families Work Activity Participation Rates

Given the sharp drop in the caseload, both in California and in the nation as a whole, the adjusted targets are much lower than the nominal required participation rates, as shown in Table 2.2. In the first year (FFY 1997), California's adjusted target for all families was 19.5 percent, well below the nominal required participation rate of 25 percent. By the third year (FFY 1999), California's adjusted target was 8.5 percent.

For the purposes of assessing penalties, achieved work activity participation rates are compared against these adjusted targets. For all families, California's participation rates have been high enough to satisfy the statutory requirement in each year, even without the caseload reduction credit. Furthermore (as shown in Table 2.2), participation rates increased from the baseline (FFY 1997) to FFY 1999, at which point 42.2 percent of all families were participating, according to the federal definition.

Since the caseload continued to decline at about 1 percent per month through FFY 2000 (ending September 2000), despite the 5 percentage point rise in the nominal target, the adjusted target falls to only 6.4 percent for 2000. With an adjusted target in single digits, unless a deep recession occurs, causing a sharp

Table 2.2

**How California Fared in Meeting Federal Work Activity
Participation-Rate Requirements
(percentage of caseloads)**

	All Families			Two-Parent Families		
	FFY 1997	FFY 1998	FFY 1999	FFY 1997	FFY 1998	FFY 1999
Federal statutory participation rate	25.0	30.0	35.0	75.0	75.0	90.0
Caseload reduction credit	5.5	12.2	26.5	34.2	42.3	53.1
Adjusted target	19.5	17.8	8.5	40.8	32.7	36.9
Participation rate	29.7	36.6	42.2	42.3	36.2	54.3

NOTES: The adjusted target is the statutorily required participation rate less the caseload reduction credit and other adjustments (not shown in the table).

SOURCE: U.S. Department of Health and Human Services, Administration for Children and Families (DHHS-ACF), at http://www.acf.dhhs.gov/programs/opre/particip/index.htm#participation. The table presents the official federal figures as of early 2001, which reflect significant revisions to official participation rates (for California and for other states) since the initial reports.

increase in the caseload, California should have little trouble satisfying the federal statutory requirement through TANF renewal (i.e., September 2002).

How California Has Fared in Meeting Two-Parent Work Activity Participation Rates

In addition to the work activities participation-rate requirements for all families, PRWORA includes separate work activities participation-rate requirements for two-parent families. Furthermore, these rates are much higher than those for all families: For FFY 1999, the rate was 90.0 percent for two-parent cases but 35.0 for all-families cases, as shown in Table 2.2. However, the two-parent caseload has declined faster than the all-families caseload. Combined with some other sizable adjustments, the caseload reduction credit for two-parent families is much larger than that for all families. The resulting adjusted target (36.9 percent for FFY 1999), while well above that for all families (8.5 percent), is far below the nominal 90 percent level required by the federal statute.

It initially appeared that California (along with 18 other states) had failed to satisfy the federal requirement for two-parent families for the first TANF year (FFY 1997), and the U.S. Department of Health and Human Services (DHHS) issued a penalty notice. California "disputed" the federal computation.[4] The

---

[4]The President's "Temporary Assistance for Needy Families Program: Third Annual Report to Congress" (August 2000) reports that in FY 1998, California was one of two states that "disputed our participation rate calculation and upon retransmission the State's data showed it met the two-parent

underlying Q5 data were reedited, and the federal government allowed the use of EDD data to impute labor earnings. On recomputation, California was found to have satisfied the statutory requirement (by 1.5 percentage points).

Since FFY 1997, the declining caseload has lowered the two-parent adjusted target. The two-parent participation rate fell from 42.3 percent in FFY 1997 to 36.2 percent in FFY 1998 (as shown in Table 2.2), but the caseload reduction credit was large enough to enable the state to meet the federal requirement (by 3.5 percentage points).

Between FFY 1998 and FFY 1999, the statutorily required participation rate increased from 75 percent to 90 percent; however, the continuing caseload decline offset one-third of that increase (4.2 percentage points). In addition, a sharp increase in the participation rate (from 36.2 percent to 54.3 percent, as shown in Table 2.2) meant that California easily (by 17.4 percentage points) satisfied the federal requirement.

Partly in response to concerns about a possible penalty, California changed its welfare program. All of the two-parent cases were moved into an SSP. The SSP could be funded with MOE dollars, but cases in an SSP are not considered to be federal TANF cases and are thus not subject to any federal participation-rate requirement. This change, also adopted by many other states, essentially removes the possibility of a penalty because of two-parent cases. Furthermore, given the current participation rates for one-parent cases and the caseload reduction credit, it probably also makes any penalty due to the federal participation-rate requirement very unlikely.

While California's caseload decline is large, it is below the national average. Thus, California's caseload reduction credit for all families (26.5 percent for FFY 1999) is smaller than the national average (35.3 percent for FFY 1999). Subtracting the caseload reduction credit from the required participation rate would yield a negative national adjusted target. Indeed, for FFY 1999, nearly half (23) of the states have a caseload reduction credit large enough to make their adjusted target negative. Because of concern that the adjusted target is no longer serving its intended role of requiring states to impose participation rates on recipients, there is serious discussion about adjusting the caseload reduction credit (perhaps with a new baseline) or raising the required participation rate as part of the renewal of the federal legislation authorizing TANF (i.e., by September 2002) for FFY 2003 and beyond.[5]

rate; therefore, it is not subject to the penalty" (http://www.lao.ca.gov/1999_reports/0899_work_rates.html). See also Hill (1999b).

[5]Haskins, Sawhill, and Weaver (2001).

How California Compares with the Rest of the Nation in Meeting Federal Work Activity Participation Rate Requirements

Table 2.3, which presents the data from Table 2.2 and adds in the national participation rate for comparison, shows that California's participation rates for all families are above the corresponding rates for the nation as a whole; California's FFY 1999 rate is 42.2 percent, and the national rate is 38.3 percent. California's two-parent participation rates are below the national average in FFY 1997 and FFY 1998, but the rates in FFY 1999 are basically the same.

Table 2.3

How California and the Rest of the Nation Fared in Meeting Federal Work Activity Participation-Rate Requirements
(percentage of caseloads)

	All Families			Two-Parent Families		
	FFY 1997	FFY 1998	FFY 1999	FFY 1997	FFY 1998	FFY 1999
Federal statutory participation rate	25.0	30.0	35.0	75.0	75.0	90.0
California						
Caseload reduction credit	5.5	12.2	26.5	34.2	42.3	53.1
Adjusted target	19.5	17.8	8.5	40.8	32.7	36.9
Participation rate	29.7	36.6	42.2	42.3	36.2	54.3
Rest of the nation	30.7	35.3	38.3	44.5	42.4	54.7

NOTES: The adjusted target is the statutorily required participation rate less caseload reduction credit and other adjustments (not shown in the table).

SOURCE: DHHS-ACF, at http://www.acf.dhhs.gov/programs/opre/particip/index.htm#participation. The table presents the official federal figures as of early 2001, which reflect significant revisions to official participation rates (for California and for other states) since the initial reports.

Near-Universal, Immediate Participation in CALWORKS WTW Activities for 32 Hours per Week

While California's all-families participation rate (42.2 percent in FFY 1999) is above the rate required by PRWORA, it is far from the goal of universal participation set out in the CalWORKs legislation. This far-from-universal participation rate appears to have several causes. First, about 13 percent of adult welfare recipients are mandatory participants according to the federal definition, but exempt according to California statute.[6] They include disabled CalWORKs recipients (not receiving federal Supplemental Security Income, SSI).

---

[6]This estimate is computed for FFY 2000 (October 1999 to September 2000) CA 237 and WTW 25 forms. It is the ratio of the sum of those with exemptions (44,740, from WTW 25) and those with good cause (7,072, from WTW 25) to the sum of adults in all other families (304,681, from CA 237) and adults in sanction who are no longer aided and are therefore not included in the CA 237 counts of

Second, about 17.0 percent of adult welfare recipients are formally noncompliant.[7] Furthermore, our fieldwork and caseworker responses to our CalWORKs Staff Survey suggest that recipients, often with the strong encouragement of management, are given multiple chances to comply before they are deemed formally noncompliant and thus counted in the above statistics.[8]

Third, some otherwise compliant participants spend sufficient time waiting for Job Club or between activities that they do not meet the standard for participation in a given month.

Fourth, some activities (e.g., treatment for substance abuse and mental health and domestic violence services; some education and training) count toward participation according to California statute, but not according to the federal regulations. Currently, the prevalence of these activities appears to be low, but it is rising, so such activities could become important in later years. Only about 3 percent of adult welfare recipients are receiving services for mental health, substance abuse, and domestic violence. Furthermore, some of these adults are also participating in other activities, and some are not participating enough hours to satisfy the federal definition of participation.

Beyond the issue of participation-rate levels are separate issues about what welfare recipients are actually participating in, how many hours they are participating (in relation to both federal and state requirements), and, for those working, employment and earnings. We discuss each of these below.

What Activities Are Welfare Recipients Participating In?

A variety of activities qualify for inclusion in the federal participation requirements. Federal statute defines participation to include work (subsidized or unsubsidized; in the public sector or the private sector; or in self-employment), as well as other activities leading to work, such as job search (but for only a limited amount of time), near-work activities (e.g., work experience, on-the-job training (OJT), CS, providing childcare for those in CS), and some forms of education. The hours requirements shown in Table 2.1 apply to hours in all

---

adults (31,165, from WTW 25). It should be noted, however, that many people—including senior officials in several counties—have expressed serious concerns about the quality of these WTW 25 data.

[7]This estimate is the ratio of the sum of those in sanction (31,165, from WTW 25) and those who are noncompliant (21,707, from WTW 25) to the sum of adults in all other families and those who are noncompliant.

[8]See Klerman et al. (2001) and Ebener and Klerman (2001).

activities, although federal regulations limit the allowable hours in some activities—job skills training directly related to employment, education directly related to employment, and satisfactory attendance at secondary school or in a course of study leading to a certificate of general equivalence may be counted only after the first 20 hours. Thus, one could, for example, meet the 25-hour all-families requirement for FY 1999 with 20 hours of work and 5 hours of training (45CFR261.31).

Both the federal and California statutes (PRWORA and CalWORKs, respectively) imply that work is the preferred activity, and Table 2.4 shows that work is overwhelmingly the most common activity. For California in FFY 1999, 84.2 percent of those participating according to the federal definition were working. This figure, however, is below the levels in earlier years. The corresponding

Table 2.4

Qualifying Participation Activities (percentage)

	All Families		
	FFY 1997	FFY 1998	FFY 1999
California			
Those participating	20.5	36.4	42.2
Work	94.7	86.9	84.2
Job search	1.9	5.5	8.2
Work experience	0.9	5.4	3.9
Education and training	2.6	4.6	10.8
Those not participating	79.5	63.6	57.8
Nation			
Those participating	25.4	33.2	35.6
Work	68.0	70.2	70.0
Job search	13.7	12.5	13.3
Work experience	86.7	17.1	16.2
Education and training	10.5	11.9	15.4
Those not participating	74.6	66.8	64.4

NOTES: Percentages for work, job search, work experience, and education and training are for those participating the required number of hours according to the federal definition of participation. Since individuals can participate in multiple activities, these percentages can sum to more than 100 percent.

SOURCE: http://www.acf.dhhs.gov/programs/opre/particip/index.htm# participation. This table presents the overall percentages as reported in the original source. Especially in the earlier years and for two-parent cases, they do not agree with the official participation rates given on the same website. Some states (including California) submitted revised Q5 files. It appears that these revised files were used to compute the revised official participation rates but that these components of participation tables were not (always) updated.

figure for the nation as a whole is still lower, only about 70 percent.[9] Put differently, among those not working, the participation rate in California is about 10 percent. Nationally, the participation rate is 14 percent.

How Many Hours Are Welfare Recipients Participating in the Activities?

The estimates above consider whether individuals participate for the number of hours required by federal statute (shown in Table 2.1): 25 hours per week, 20 hours per week for those with a child under six years of age in FFY 1999. The CalWORKs statute requires even more hours than the federal statute, 32 hours as of July 1, 1999,[10] and counties had the option of requiring 32 hours even earlier.[11] Most counties took advantage of this option. With a higher number of required hours, the corresponding participation rates will be lower.

Figure 2.1 plots hours of participation as reported in the Q5 data among one-parent and two-parent families in FFY 1999.[12] About 55 percent of one-parent families and 80 percent of two-parent families participate at least one hour in a given month. This percentage is roughly consistent with the county WTW 25 filings.[13]

The number of cases participating enough hours to meet statutory guidelines is smaller than the number participating at all. Federal statute requires 25 hours per week (fewer hours for women with children under six). At a 25-hours-per-week cutoff, participation rates are lower, about 28 percent and 57 percent for one-parent and two-parent cases in California, respectively. At the 32 hours per week required by the CalWORKs statute, participation is lower still, about 20 percent and 51 percent for one-parent and two-parent cases, respectively.

---

[9]These estimates are computed as the ratio of those participating according to the federal requirement and reporting any work to the complement of people not participating.

[10]See AB 1542 11322.8. Starting January 1, 1998, 20 hours per week; July 1, 1998, 26 hours per week; and July 1, 1999, 32 hours per week; and "a county retains the option to require all recipients or individual recipients to participate in welfare-to-work activities in excess of the minimum number of hours specified in this subdivision, up to 32 hours per week." See LAO (1/23/98), which recommends aligning the CalWORKs hourly participation requirement with the lower TANF requirement.

[11]See Table 5.1 in Klerman et al. (2001) for a depiction of how the 24 study counties in the evaluation made their choices about when to implement the 32-hour requirement.

[12]Corresponding to the definition of hours for a two-parent case, the two-parent estimates include hours for both adults. Figures for the last quarter of FFY 1999 (after the state 32-hour requirement was in place in every county) are similar; in fact, they are slightly lower.

[13]The earliest WTW 25 that has been publicly released is for October 1999 (the month after the end of the period covered by this figure). It shows a 51 percent participation rate (262,072 enrollees and 134,562 participants).

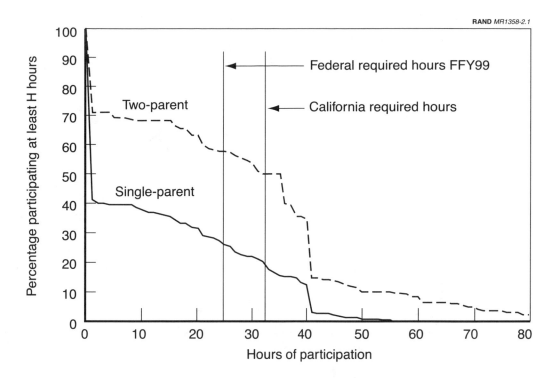

SOURCE: RAND tabulations from FFY 1999 Q5 microdata file.

Figure 2.1—Hours of Participation, One-Parent and Two-Parent Cases

Of Those Current Welfare Recipients Who Are Working, How Much Are They Working?

A longer historical perspective would help in understanding the determinants of these participation rates. Unfortunately, consistently defined participation-rate data do not appear to be available for the pre-PRWORA period. However, as shown in Table 2.4, the overwhelming share of participation is work, and consistently defined information on employment and earnings is available from employer filings to the Unemployment Insurance (UI) system.[14]

Figure 2.2 shows the percentage of one-parent-family welfare recipients with any earnings reported to the UI system. The UI reports include total earnings, so we can use them to construct a proxy for hours worked. We derive our proxy by dividing total quarterly earnings into the then-current California minimum wage

---

[14]These data are also known as the MEDS-EDD match. See Appendix B and Klerman et al. (2000) for a more complete description of these data.

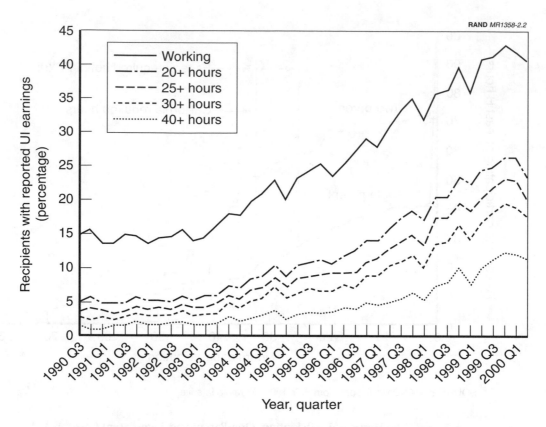

SOURCE: RAND tabulations from the 5 percent MEDS-EDD match file.

NOTE: Hours worked are imputed by dividing quarterly earnings by 260 or 416 hours at the then-minimum wage of $5.75 (as of late 2000). We use this wage even in all years (even for the period before September 1997 when the applicable statutory minimum wage was lower). This estimate is likely to be too high. (See the discussion in text.)

Figure 2.2—Employment and Earnings per Quarter for Current One-Parent-Family Welfare Recipients

of $5.75 an hour (and dividing by 13 weeks per quarter).[15] We then plot the percentage of current welfare recipients with earnings consistent with hours greater than cutoff values of 20, 25, 30, and 40 hours per week. Since some (and probably a growing fraction) earn more than the minimum wage, this proxy is an overestimate (and any increase is probably overestimated).

The results for one-parent families are striking. In the early 1990s (when required hours were lower and exemptions were broader), only about 15 percent of welfare recipients had any UI earnings; less than 5 percent had earnings

---

[15]See Appendix C for a discussion of the potential errors in the proxy. Note that $5.75 was the minimum wage through the end of calendar year 2000. As of January 1, 2001, the California minimum wage rose to $6.25.

consistent with even 20 hours per week. Then, beginning in early 1993, total employment and employment above each of the hours-worked cutoffs exploded. Total employment increased nearly linearly from about 15 percent in 1993 to over 40 percent in late 1999; employment above the 25-hour-per-week equivalent increased from less than 5 percent in 1993 to nearly 20 percent in late 1999; and full-time employment (40 hours per week) increased from about 2 percent in 1993 to about 12 percent.[16] The dip at the very end of the data is probably due to technical considerations.

Figure 2.3 presents equivalent results for two-parent families. The levels are higher, but the trends are similar: steady and low rates of employment through about 1993 and an explosion of work thereafter.

Possible Explanations for Descriptive Findings

Having described the levels of participation and employment, we next consider their determinants. How do welfare policies and other factors affect the differences in participation and employment across states? What role have welfare policies and other factors played in the increase in participation and employment through time?

In this section, we review the evidence on the role of the factors shown in Figure 1.1 and discussed in Section 1. We first discuss the impact of county CalWORKs programs, then examine the effect of caseload composition, pre-CalWORKs reforms and CalWORKs legislation changes to the benefit structure, other CalWORKs legislative changes, and the economy. The second impact analysis report will include additional analyses.

The Effects of County Welfare Programs

The available evidence suggests that some of the increase in participation rates in the post-CalWORKs period resulted from county WTW programs. We review

---

[16]Two statistical issues should be considered in interpreting these figures. First, the sawtooth pattern of rates being below trend every fourth quarter (including the last quarter plotted on the figures) is evidence of seasonality; employment is lowest in the winter.

Second, the declines in rates in the most recent two quarters are probably not real. The rates in these quarters tend to be lower than those in the quarters immediately prior because of incomplete reporting. Previous patterns suggest that total reported earnings for these quarters will rise as employers have more time to report earnings for them. We have made no formal attempt to control for this incomplete reporting.

We will consider more formal approaches to dealing with this dip in the last quarter in the second report.

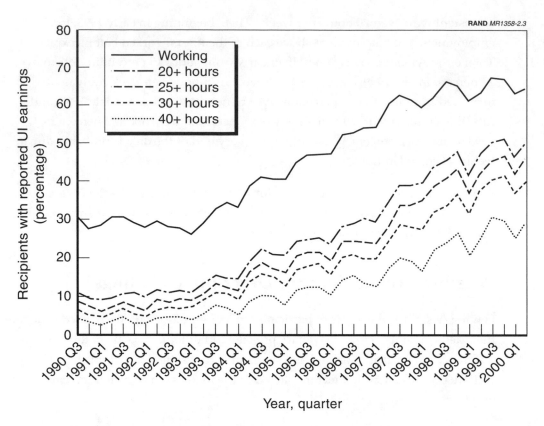

RAND *MR1358-2.3*

SOURCE: RAND tabulations from the 5 percent MEDS-EDD match file.

NOTE: Hours worked are imputed by dividing quarterly earnings for the case (i.e., both husband and wife) by 260 or 416 hours at the California minimum wage for 2000, $5.75 per hour (as of late 2000). We use this wage even in all years (even for the period before September 1997 when the applicable statutory minimum wage was lower). This estimate is likely to be too high (see the discussion in Appendix C). The underlying numbers and separate calculations for most counties are available at http://www.rand.org/CalWORKs/IA-1.

Figure 2.3—Total Employment and Earnings per Quarter for Current Two-Parent-Family Welfare Recipients

the timing of program roll-out in more detail at the beginning of Section 3 (on caseloads). Here, we note that in FFY 1997, California's WTW program was underfunded, and—despite the 1995 GAIN legislation's reorientation of the program toward a more work-first approach—most counties still had education-and-training-focused GAIN programs. In FFY 1998 and FFY 1999, the CalWORKs program was rolled out and the existing cases were processed through the new and better-funded program model. Specifically, large numbers of recipients went through Job Club in late 1998 and early 1999, and nearly immediate Job Club has become almost universal for new entrants. The goal of programs such as Job Club is to increase participation and employment. Counties report that among those who participate, a high proportion find jobs while enrolled in or shortly after Job Club. This claim is consistent with MDRC's random-assignment studies of WTW programs in selected California counties (Freedman et al., 2000) and elsewhere (Riccio, Friedlander, and Freedman, 1994) that find that such work-first WTW programs raise participation rates and employment rates.

Nevertheless, it seems unlikely that all of the increase in participation or employment is attributable to program effects. Compared to programs in the post-CalWORKs period, WTW programs in the pre-CalWORKs era were small and funding was relatively stable, yet employment rates rose dramatically. Furthermore, county WTW programs were still ramping up at least through the end of FFY 1998 (i.e., October 1998).

The Effects of the Composition of California's Welfare Caseload

Although it is not one of the causal factors called out in Section 1, the composition of California's welfare caseload plays a role in explaining why California's all-families participation rate is higher than that of the nation as a whole. The size of California's two-parent caseload makes that comparison an imperfect measure of California's relative success in involving recipients in work activities. California has a very large two-parent program,[17] and two-parent cases have higher participation rates than one-parent cases.[18] This raises California's all-families rate relative to that in other states (which have a smaller fraction of two-parent cases).

A comparison of California's pure one-parent work activities participation rate to that of the nation as a whole provides further insights. Unfortunately, DHHS does not publish one-parent rates. However, working from the Q5 data for California, we estimate a one-parent rate of 37.2 percent for FFY 1999, considerably lower than the 42.2 percent rate for all families shown in Table 2.2.[19] For the nation as a whole, we estimate a one-parent rate of 36.2 percent in FFY 1999, also lower than the 38.3 percent rate shown in Table 2.2.[20] Thus, while California's all-families participation rate is 3.9 percentage points higher than

---

[17]In FFY 1998, over half (54 percent) of all two-parent cases in the nation were in California, although California has only 18 percent of the nation's total cases. Put differently, 16 percent of California's cases were two-parent cases; in the rest of the nation, these cases make up only 3 percent of the total.

[18]Table 2.2 shows higher participation rates among two-parent cases than among all-families cases. Since all-families cases include both two-parent and one-parent cases, two-parent cases must have higher participation rates than one-parent cases. Furthermore, the higher participation rates are achieved subject to a higher hours requirement. Participation rates for two-parent families are even higher when measured against the lower one-parent/all-families hours requirement.

[19]See Appendix C for details.

[20]See Appendix C for details.

that of the nation as a whole, our estimated pure one-parent participation rates differ by only 1.0 percentage point. Although California's all-families rate is higher than the national average, it appears that most of that difference results from the higher fraction of two-parent families in California's caseload (which are therefore included in the computation of California's all-families participation rate).

The Effects of Pre-CalWORKs Reforms and CalWORKs Legislative Changes to the Benefit Structure

It seems likely that the pre-CalWORKs and CalWORKs changes to the benefit structure explain some of the increase in employment (and thus participation over time) and also cause California's employment rates to be higher than they would be if California adopted the benefit structure of other states. Some of these changes are likely to be behavioral—people on aid work more—and some are likely to be compositional—some working families can remain on welfare because of the changes to the benefit structure.

Prior to 1993, the structure of welfare benefits implied that welfare recipients kept little of their earnings. Not surprisingly, given the small financial rewards of working, few worked. As noted in Section 1, fill-the-gap budgeting adopted in 1992 and the Work Pays reforms initiated in 1993 changed the benefit structure, allowing recipients to keep more of their earnings. These changes were augmented in the CalWORKs legislation, so that today a recipient keeps the first $225 of her earnings and half of her earnings above that level up to the point where the household is income-ineligible for aid. The federal EITC further increases current welfare recipients' incentive to work. Evidence from national random-assignment evaluations of similar changes to the benefit structure (e.g., Berlin, 2000; Blank, Card, and Robbins, 2000) and econometric evaluations of the federal EITC are consistent with the idea that these policies play a major role (e.g., Hotz and Scholz, 2000; Meyer and Rosenbaum, 1999, 2000). We note, however, that CDSS's random-assignment evaluation of the Work Pays reforms found few statistically significant effects and suggested that part of the problem was that recipients were not being informed of the changes (Meyers, Glaser, and MacDonald, 1998).

Changes to the benefit structure affect employment among current recipients and participation rates in two different ways. First, there is a behavioral effect: Because a recipient can take home more of her earnings, she works more. Second, there is a mechanical effect. A higher earned-income disregard and a lower BRR imply that a recipient remains eligible for cash assistance at a higher level of total earnings. The structure of benefits in California implies that a woman with two children must work full time at about $8.75 an hour to be income-ineligible for CalWORKs. In many other states, full-time or even half-time work at the minimum wage makes a family income-ineligible for cash assistance. Thus, recipients who in another state would be income-ineligible for cash assistance remain eligible for, and often remain on, welfare in California.

Using the Q5 data, we can simulate the magnitude of the effect of benefit structure on the participation rate. Our analysis focuses on those working sufficient hours to be income-ineligible in other states (half-time to full-time at the federal minimum wage, $5.15 per hour). Because these recipients are working more than 25 hours per week, they appear in both the numerator and the denominator of the federal participation rate, raising the rate over what it would be in a state with a lower level of maximum earnings. We can tabulate the fraction of California welfare cases with earnings high enough to make them income-ineligible in other states.[21] Assuming that every such person was participating according to the federal definition, we can then compute the effect on the participation rate.

The full results of the simulation are presented in Appendix D. Here, we summarize the results. If, as an example, California were to adopt Alabama's benefit structure, the mechanical model implies that approximately 24.9 percent of its caseload would be income-ineligible and the participation rate would fall from 42.2 percent to 23.0 percent. This simple simulation ignores the behavioral response to the benefit structure. We can use conventional labor-supply models and estimates to make a rough correction for such behavioral effects (Ashenfelter, 1983; Blank, Card, and Robbins, 2000). Those behavioral responses will, in general, lead to a caseload decline somewhat larger than that resulting from the mechanical response.[22] The behavioral response magnifies the effect, so

---

[21]This calculation implicitly ignores interstate differences in the cost of living and in the level of wages.

[22]The analysis is similar to the conventional analysis of the EITC in reverse. Cases in California with earnings just above the cutoff in the other state would certainly not collect welfare in the other state, where the benefit level is lower, causing them to work more; and the BRR is lower (on welfare in California, they face a 50 percent BRR; off welfare in the other state, they face a 0 BRR). For these people, the mechanical simulation is exactly correct.

Cases in California with earnings just below the cutoff in the other state would choose either to continue to collect welfare or to work more and stop collecting welfare. The lower benefit induces them to work more, possibly making them income-ineligible; the higher BRR (California's 50 percent rate compared to BRRs of 67 percent or higher) causes them to want to work less. For these cases, the mechanical effect may be too small (in absolute value); the net behavioral effect is a small increase in work, causing some of these recipients (who remained eligible according to the mechanical simulation) to become income-ineligible. Therefore, the behavioral model yields a decrease in the caseload and in the participation rate that is larger than that of the mechanical model, but not much larger.

that, for the example of Alabama, the caseload declines slightly more (26.5 percent) and the participation rate also declines slightly more (to 21.4 percent).

Alabama has one of the lowest benefit levels. Therefore, the estimated impact of Alabama's benefit structure on California's caseload and participation rate are among the largest for any single state. Estimates weighting all 50 states, where the weights are the caseloads, indicate that if California were to adopt the "average" benefit structure of other states, its participation rate would be about 8.3 percentage points lower.

The Effects of Other CalWORKs Legislative Changes

Other features of the CalWORKs legislation may also lead to lower participation rates. Some states (e.g., Wisconsin and Wyoming) have achieved much higher participation rates, apparently (at least in part) by mandating some specific activity (e.g., CS) immediately and continuously while adults remain on aid and by making participation a condition of receipt of cash assistance. By contrast, California does not require a specific activity (CS) until 24 months after signing a WTW plan, and in practice, this often means 30 or more months after first receipt of cash assistance. Furthermore, California's sanction for failure to participate is smaller than that of many other states ($125 out of $645 for a family of three), because it applies only to adults.[23] The conciliation process and a reluctance to sanction in some counties and on the part of some caseworkers also makes the penalty less sure and thus the incentive to participate smaller.

The Effects of the Economy

Improvements in employment among welfare recipients pre-date CalWORKs, stretching back to 1993. We have already noted that the Work Pays reforms and the expansion of the EITC appear to explain some of the increase. It also seems likely that some of the increase in employment results from the fact that the improving economy makes jobs easier to find, thus raising employment rates. The timing is consistent with that explanation. The evaluation for the coming year will explore the extent to which the improving economy explains higher employment rates.

---

[23]Nonexempt, Region 1, as of July 2000.

3. The Caseload

Welfare programs exist to provide a minimal level of support for children. Among the changes brought about by welfare reform was the addition of a complementary goal of "reducing dependency," i.e., cutting the caseload. The relative importance of these two goals—providing a minimal level of support to poor children and reducing dependency—is a matter of considerable debate, to which we return at the end of this section.

Regardless of the relative weight attached to these goals, the level and composition of the caseload are key indicators of outcomes under CalWORKs, and they provide important insights into the effects of CalWORKs' policies and programs. Beyond being a key measure of dependency, the size and composition of the caseload drive total aid payments and the staffing levels needed to administer the grant and provide WTW services.

This section describes trends in the caseload. We first describe the overall trends (in the aggregate) and then disaggregate them for several different subgroups. The path of California's caseload decline is then compared with that in other states. The section concludes with a preliminary discussion of the evidence on the causes of the trends. We examine the factors identified in the model in Section 1 in explaining the caseload results in California and in explaining those results in relation to the rest of the nation.[1]

Overview of Descriptive Findings

The basic story is straightforward and therefore central to the evolution of the CalWORKs program. Since a peak in March of 1995, the caseload has fallen approximately 1 percent per month; as of late 2000, it had fallen to a level nearly half its peak. This decline is unprecedented and broad-based. In addition, when we adjust the caseload decline to account for changes in population, we find that the decline in the per-capita caseload was even larger than the gross caseload decline, and when we account for composition shifts in the population, the composition-adjusted decline is larger still.

---

[1]We defer until the second report detailed consideration of the differential caseload decline in California's counties.

However, in comparison with other states, the decline in California is smaller than the average decline in the rest of the nation and much smaller than that in some other states. Although there are various ways to make the comparison, the basic story is invariant. First, California's caseload peaked a year later than that in the rest of the nation. Second, California's increase to its peak caseload was much larger than that of the rest of the nation. Third, California's caseload decline was much smaller than the decline in the rest of the nation. Fourth, the decline was not homogeneous. Finally, California's population growth was slightly larger than the percentage increase for the nation, accounting in part for its slower decrease in caseload.

Caseload Trends in California

As mentioned above. We take both an aggregated and a disaggregated view of the caseload trends in California. Here, we break the aggregate view into two parts, looking first at the overall picture from March 1990 to March 2000, then breaking the overall picture down into a series of subperiods.

Aggregate Statewide Trends

The recent history of the caseload in California can be divided into two phases, starting in about March 1995. As Figure 3.1 shows, the caseload increased sharply, starting in about 1990 and peaking in March 1995. In March 1990, the caseload stood at about 656,544. Exactly five years later, it stood at 932,345, an increase of 42 percent.[2]

After March 1995, this pattern reverses. Exactly five years later in March 2000, the caseload stood at about 567,549, a decline of 39 percent. Furthermore, the caseload decline has continued, and in October 2000, it stood at 529,248, for a decline from the peak of 43.2 percent. The pace of the decline has slowed slightly

---

[2]We adopt these March dates for convenience and the five-year intervals for symmetry. Choosing the same calendar month in different years provides a rough correction for the seasonal patterns in the time series.

The data in this discussion are from the CA 237 form and refer to "Cases receiving cash grant ($10 more)" during the calendar month. These CA 237 data are based on the official county reports to the state and are used by the state in compiling some of its filings to the federal government.

CA 237 contains only aggregate data, so longitudinal analyses are not possible. Thus, CA 237 data can only be disaggregated by month, county, program (see below), and adults versus children. Furthermore, the coding of the program changes through time.

To complement these CA 237-based estimates, we also provide tabulations from the individual-level data in the MEDS file that identify individuals and cases. However, they are not the source of the official caseload statistics and there are some divergences (mostly small) between the official counts from CA 237 and the MEDS file.

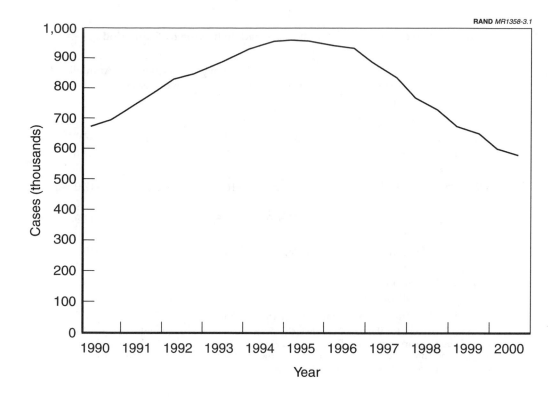

Figure 3.1—Total Caseload in California

to about 10 percent per year, down from the peak year-over-year decline of 14 percent between February 1997 and February 1998.

Table 3.1 indicates the timing of the decline. The available data are divided into seven periods that we will use throughout this part of the analysis. Here, we summarize the status of CalWORKs programs during the periods and the magnitude of the decline. In the discussion of causation later in this section, we relate the timing of the decline to the timing of the roll-out of the components of the CalWORKs program and consider the implications of the timing of the two sequences of events for the likely effect of the CalWORKs reforms on the caseload decline.

The first period covers the five years from March 1990 to March 1995. The caseload increased 42.0 percent during this period, an annual rate of 7.0 percent.

The second period covers the interval from March 1995 to the passage of federal welfare reform (PRWORA) in August 1996; however, to align the caseload changes with SFYs, we have set the break in the periods to July 1996. Over this interval, the caseload dropped 5.4 points, a 4.0 percent decline per year.

Table 3.1

Percentage Change in the Caseload, Statewide by Subperiod

Date	Label	Cases	% Change from Peak	% Change Over Period	Annualized % Change
3/90	Pre-reform baseline (5 years pre-peak)	656,544	29.6	—	—
3/95	Caseload peak	932,345	0.0	42.0	7.0
7/96	Passage of PRWORA (8/97)	882,164	-5.4	-5.4	-4.0
7/97	Passage of CalWORKs (8/99)	776,022	-16.8	-12.0	-12.0
7/98	End of first year of CalWORKs	675,540	-27.5	-12.9	-12.9
7/99	End of second year of CalWORKs	606,533	-34.9	-10.2	-10.2
7/00	End of third year of CalWORKs	545,647	-41.5	-10.0	-10.0
10/00	Most recent available data	529,248	-43.2	-3.0	-11.5

NOTE: Except for the first two rows, the dates are chosen to align with SFYs (i.e., July–June). Labels are approximate. Percentage changes are from each date to the next. Annualized change is the annualized percentage change in the caseload. Annualizing corrects for the different lengths of the first two periods.

The third period covers the next year, July 1996 to July 1997. This is approximately the interval between the passage of PRWORA and the passage of welfare reform in California (CalWORKs) in August 1997. During this interval, there was considerable publicity about the changing welfare system, but no new regulations went into effect in California, funding levels did not change significantly, and new CalWORKs programs were still a year or more away. Over this year, the caseload dropped to 16.8 percent below its peak, a 12.0 percent rate of decline per year.

The fourth period covers the first year of CalWORKs, July 1997 to July 1998. During this interval, there was more publicity about the changing welfare system, and some of the policy changes—the new benefit structure and time limits—went into effect. For CWDs, this was primarily a period of strategic planning and capacity building, although some counties and caseworkers began to aggressively inform recipients that the old world of time-unlimited welfare had ended. However, our fieldwork for the process analysis (e.g., Zellman et al., 1999a,b; Klerman et al., 2000) suggests that county WTW programs did not change much. Toward the end of the period, counties started to call recipients into welfare offices to "enroll" them in CalWORKs, but most enrollment appears to have happened toward the end of calendar year 1998 (up against the statutory deadline of December 31, 1998), i.e., in the second year of CalWORKs. Over this year, the caseload dropped to 27.5 percent below its peak, a 12.9 percent rate of decline per year.

The fifth period covers the second year of CalWORKs, July 1998 to July 1999. During this interval, recipients started to interact with the changing WTW system. They were enrolled, and this enrollment often involved a face-to-face meeting with a caseworker in which the new rules and the new expectations were conveyed. In most counties, this process was completed by about the statutory deadline (December 31, 1998), but only through a surge of enrollments late in the calendar year (including some by mail, rather than in person).

After recipients completed enrollment, they were assigned to Job Club as slots became available. In most counties, Job Club began in volume around the beginning of the fiscal year (i.e., July 1998), and approximately a year was required to handle the backlog of existing cases. Counties report high job-finding rates among those who participated in Job Club. They also report high noncompliance rates. After encouraging participation through intensive casework, counties turned to the formal noncompliance process and, as necessary, sanctions. Initial no-shows who later participated contributed to the continuing Job Club surge at least through the end of the fiscal year (i.e., July 1999) (Zellman et al., 1999a,b; Klerman et al., 2000). Toward the end of the period, counties began to move recipients who had not found jobs into assessment and then post-assessment activities. Over the year, the caseload dropped to 34.9 percent below its peak, a 10.2 percent rate of decline per year.

The sixth period covers the third year of CalWORKs, July 1999 to July 2000. During this interval, county WTW programs moved into steady-state operation. Most of the backlog of existing cases had gone through Job Club. During this period, they moved through assessment and into post-assessment WTW activities. New cases were processed. New staff and contractors were coming on-line, providing more intensive case management and specialized services. CWD expenditures were rising rapidly. Counties moved to refine and improve their operations and processes. During this year, the caseload dropped to 41.5 percent below its peak, a 10.0 percent rate of decline per year.

The final period includes the most recent months for which we have data. The caseload decline continued through the early months of SFY 2000–2001 at an annualized rate of 11.5 percent. At least up to this point, there is little evidence of a slowing of the rate of caseload decline.

Disaggregated Trends by Subgroups

How different is the story when we disaggregate the overall statewide trends into subgroups, in this case by regions of the state, by program type, by race/ethnicity, and by urbanicity?

Regions of the State. The magnitude of the decline varies across the regions of the state and individual counties. Figure 3.2 shows the decline for the five regions—Northern California, Coastal/Bay Area, Central Valley, Southern California (less Los Angeles County), and Los Angeles County.[3] Table 3.2 presents detailed results for each of the regions. Appendix E provides the full results for each of the 58 counties.

In the five years preceding the caseload peak, the caseload increased fastest—by over 50 percent—in Los Angeles County and the rest of Southern California (50.4 percent and 54.6 percent, respectively). The increase was smaller in the Central

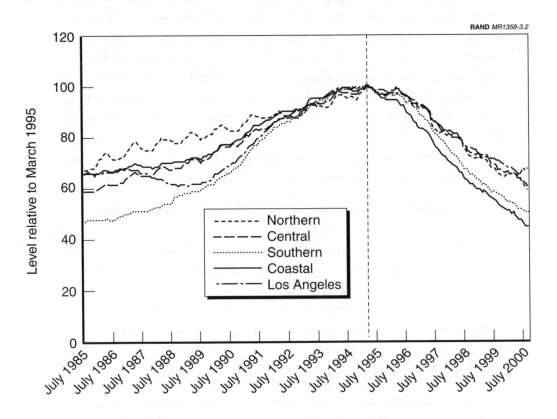

Figure 3.2—Total AFDC/TANF Caseload by Region

---

[3]We treat Los Angeles County as its own region both because of its size (about 40 percent of the state's caseload) and its sometimes divergent trends.

Table 3.2

Caseload Decline by Region

Region/County	Caseload, September 2000	% of State	Change (percent)							
			3/90- 3/95	3/95- 7/96	7/97- 7/97	7/97- 7/98	7/98- 7/99	7/99- 7/00	7/00- 9/00	From Peak
Statewide	537,908	100.0	42.0	-5.4	-12.0	-12.9	-10.2	-10.0	-1.4	-42.3
Northern California	22,629	4.2	18.7	-4.2	-13.4	-8.9	-10.9	-9.5	-3.4	-41.1
Central Valley	122,051	22.7	31.0	-4.3	-10.6	-10.6	-9.8	-10.1	-1.8	-39.1
Coastal/Bay Area	62,096	11.5	30.3	-9.3	-15.8	-16.2	-13.5	-17.0	-3.3	-55.5
Southern California	118,665	22.1	54.6	-6.4	-13.3	-16.8	-12.9	-13.5	-1.0	-49.6
Los Angeles	212,467	39.5	50.4	-3.8	-10.3	-11.0	-7.4	-5.6	-0.6	-33.3

SOURCE: County CA 237 submissions.

Valley and the Bay Area, less than one-third (31.0 percent and 30.3 percent, respectively); and smallest in the Northern part of the state (18.7 percent).

The patterns have been quite different since the peak (rightmost column in Table 3.2). The declines in the Bay Area and Southern California are larger (55.5 percent and 49.6 percent, respectively) than the statewide decline (42.3 percent), and Los Angeles County has a significantly smaller decline (33.3 percent).

These patterns have been relatively stable. In almost every subperiod, the declines in the Coastal/Bay Area and Southern California regions have been well above the state average, and the declines in Los Angeles County have been well below. If anything, the declines in Los Angeles County are diverging even more (i.e., they are smaller relative to the rest of the state) in the later period (July 1998–July 1999, 7.4 percent versus 10.2 percent; July 1999–July 2000, 5.6 percent versus 10.0 percent).

Program Type. Under AFDC (and until October 1999), California's caseload was officially broken down into two parts, family group (FG) and unemployed parent (UP). Under CalWORKs (since October 1999), the caseload has been officially broken down into three parts: all other families (one-parent), two-parent families, and zero-parent families (child only).[4] Some of the new child-only group had formerly been FG and some had formerly been UP. As of October 2000, one-parent families made up about 60 percent of the caseload (319,574

---

[4]Official case types changed in October 1999 with the creation of the SSP for two-parent families and the simultaneous creation of an official zero-parent group. See ACL 99-33, *Revision of the CalWORKs Cash Grant Caseload Movement and Expenditures Report (CA 237 CalWORKs)*, April 29, 1999 (for use as of July 1, 1999).

cases), two-parent families made up 11 percent (57,394), and child-only cases made up 29 percent (152,280).

The change in the official definitions obscures some of the time trends. From the individual-level MEDS data, we have created a consistent-through-time classification based on the number of adults in a case.[5] Table 3.3 presents the rates of change in the caseload by number of adults, as well as by race/ethnicity and urbanization. Each categorization is discussed below.

In the five years before the peak, caseload growth was not concentrated in the one-parent group, which represents most of the cases. The increase in this group, while substantial (31.3 percent), was considerably smaller than that of the caseload as a whole. The difference is the much faster caseload growth of zero-adult households (51.2 percent) and two-parent households (68.3 percent). This pattern is consistent with nationwide trends (see, e.g., Blank, 2001).

Table 3.3

Caseload Change by Subgroup
(percentage)

	% Change						
	3/90-3/95	3/95-7/96	7/96-7/97	7/97-7/98	7/98-7/99	7/99-7/00	From Peak
Statewide	46.1	-2.0	-9.3	-11.5	-11.2	-10.5	-38.7
Number of adults							
None	51.2	0.4	-3.0	-0.3	3.3	-1.7	-3.7
1	31.3	-2.5	-11.0	-15.9	-19.0	-16.3	-51.3
2 or more	68.3	-4.9	-16.1	-20.3	-20.7	-19.2	-60.4
Race/ethnicity							
White	19.8	-3.2	-9.0	-13.0	-16.2	-9.8	-43.8
Black	14.9	-2.5	-6.4	-7.7	-8.6	-11.5	-33.1
Latino	91.5	0.2	-10.9	-12.1	-8.9	-9.7	-36.4
Other	27.9	-6.0	-8.5	-11.6	-10.3	-13.8	-42.9
Urbanization							
Rural	41.3	-4.4	-11.3	-12.2	-10.0	-10.1	-40.8
Mixed	35.5	-6.0	-12.4	-13.6	-10.7	-12.9	-45.7
Urban	37.9	-7.5	-14.4	-15.6	-13.9	-14.4	-51.7
L.A. County	50.4	-3.8	-10.3	-11.0	-7.4	-5.6	-33.3

SOURCE: RAND tabulations from the MEDS micro-data file.

NOTE: The MEDS data come from a different data system than the official CA 237 caseload figures, so these figures do not align exactly with the official CA 237 caseload figures (e.g., for L.A. County).

---

[5]See Appendix C for details.

The patterns in the decline since the peak are quite different. Since March 1995, the caseload decline is largest for two-parent cases (60.4 percent versus 38.7 percent). The one-parent decline is only slightly smaller than the two-parent decline (51.3 percent), and the zero-parent caseload has barely declined at all (3.7 percent). Finally, this pattern of largest declines for two-parent families and smallest declines for zero-parent families is consistent across each of the subperiods.

Race/Ethnicity. There is also some divergence by race/ethnicity, as shown in Table 3.3. From March 1990 to March 1995, the caseload increase was smallest for blacks and whites (14.9 percent and 19.8 percent, respectively), larger for other (primarily Asians, 27.9 percent), and largest (and much larger) for Latinos (91.5 percent). For the decline from March 1995 to October 2000, the differences are small: largest for whites (43.8 percent), followed by Asians (42.9 percent), Latinos (36.4 percent), and blacks (33.1 percent).

Relative to the differences in the caseload decline in the pre-peak period, the differences in later periods across groups are small and the patterns are not consistent across subperiods. In particular, for SFY 1999–2000, caseload declines for whites, which had been above the statewide average, are below the statewide average, while those for blacks, which had been below the statewide average, are now above it.

Urbanization. Compared to the striking variation by region, program, and race/ethnicity, the variation by degree of urbanization is small.[6] We have already noted that the increase in the caseload was largest for Los Angeles County (50.4 percent, according to the MEDS data used for these tabulations). The other groupings are in a narrow band, with the largest increase in the rural counties (41.3 percent), the smallest increase in the mixed counties (35.5 percent), and intermediate increases in the other urban counties (i.e., excluding Los Angeles County, which has about one-third of the state's caseload, 37.9 percent).

The patterns are similar since the peak. Excluding the decline in Los Angeles County (where the decline is 33.3 percent), the decline is smallest in the rural counties (40.8 percent), largest in the urban counties (51.7 percent), and intermediate in the mixed counties (45.7). Furthermore, these rankings are relatively stable. The decline is always largest in the urban counties (excluding Los Angeles County), and, as noted earlier, smallest in Los Angeles County.

---

[6]See Appendix C for the classification of the counties by urbanization.

The Effects of Changes in Population and Composition on California's Caseload

So far, this discussion has focused on the total caseload, which drives program costs. However, to understand the causes of changes in the caseload, it is useful to consider also the per-capita caseload and the composition-adjusted per-capita caseload. Increases in the state population alone will drive up the caseload, even if the probability that an individual is on welfare remains constant. Similarly, changes in the composition of the population could increase the caseload, even if the probability that an individual with given characteristics is on welfare remained unchanged.

California's population increased over this period, especially later in the period. If recipiency rates had remained constant, then the 6 percent increase in the state's population between calendar year 1995 and calendar year 2000 would have been expected to yield a 6 percent increase in the caseload. Put differently, the per-capita decline in the caseload was even larger than the gross caseload decline, 45 percent versus 39 percent.

Not only has the state's total population grown, the composition of the population has shifted toward groups that are more likely to receive welfare. California has seen a large growth in the fraction of its population composed of young Hispanics. Younger women are more likely to have children, and Hispanics, having less education and poorer labor-market opportunities, are more likely to need welfare. If rates had remained constant, this composition shift would have yielded a further 3 percent increase in the caseload. Put differently, the decline in the composition-adjusted caseload was 48 percent (rather than the gross decline of 39 percent or the per-capita decline of 45 percent).[7] Thus, rather than explaining the caseload decline, changes in the size and composition of the population further increase its magnitude.

---

[7]These estimates are calculated using the RAND 1 percent MEDS microdata file and population data from the California Department of Finance to calculate welfare recipiency rates. The rates are calculated by race (4 groups—white, black, Latino, other), age (10 groups—ages 0-49 grouped in five-year increments), gender, county, and year.

In this analysis, we hold welfare recipiency rates constant at 2000 levels and examine the impact of population. To test the robustness of our estimates, we performed the same analysis holding recipiency rates constant at 1995 levels. The results are quite similar, suggesting that population changes would have led to an 8 percent increase in caseloads, with composition shifts accounting for one-fourth of the growth.

California's Caseload Trends Relative to the Rest of the Nation

In this subsection, we compare California's caseload decline to that in the nation as a whole. Figure 3.3 shows the national caseload decline and the decline in California.

Table 3.4 presents several calculations of the relative caseload decline, using the official federal statistics adjusted for establishment of an SSP for two-parent families in California and other states. It compares California against the nation and against the nation less California. It considers the change relative to the peak in California, in the nation, and in the nation less California.

The basic story is invariant with the series used. First, California's caseload peaked a year later than the caseload in the rest of the nation: March 1995 in California versus March 1994 for the rest of the nation.

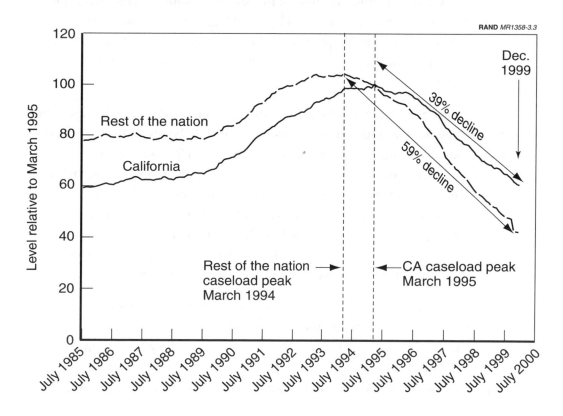

SOURCE: State filings to U.S. DHHS-ACF.

Figure 3.3—Caseload Decline: California versus the Rest of the Nation

Table 3.4

Caseload Decline by Period: U.S., California, U.S. Less California

	Caseload Total (in millions)			% Change from Baseline to Peak			% Change from Peak to Recent		
	U.S.	U.S.-CA	CA	U.S.	U.S.-CA	CA	U.S.	U.S.-CA	CA
3/90 baseline	3.94	3.29	0.66	0	0	0	—	—	—
3/94 U.S. and U.S.-CA peak	5.04	4.12	0.92	28	25	40	-56	-59	-38
3/95 CA peak	4.88	3.95	0.93	24	20	42	-54	-58	-39
12/99 recent	2.24	1.67	0.57	—	—	—	0	0	0

SOURCE: U.S.-CA caseload numbers: U.S. DHHS. CA caseload numbers: CA 237.

NOTE: Caseload estimates for CA add back in California's two-parent caseload and an approximation to the two-parent caseloads of other states with SSPs (which is not included in official federal TANF figures because cases in SSPs are not federal TANF cases).

Second, California's caseload increase from March 1990 to the peak—however defined—was much larger than that of the rest of the nation. As we have noted, California's increase to its peak was 42 percent (see the middle panel, third column, fourth row). In the rest of the nation, the increase from March 1990 to the national peak in March 1994 was only 25 percent, a difference of 17 percentage points.

Third, California's caseload decline—according to any of the three datings of the caseload peak—was much smaller than the decline in the rest of the nation. The magnitude of the difference depends on where the decline is measured from. The divergence between California and the nation is smallest when measured from California's caseload peak—39 percent in California versus 58 percent in the rest of the nation, or 19 percentage points. If the decline is measured relative to the caseload peak in the rest of the nation, California's decline is smaller (38 percent vs. 39 percent) and the national decline is larger (59 percent versus 58 percent), so the difference is even larger—21 percentage points.

Fourth, it is important to note that the decline was not homogeneous in the rest of the nation. The average decline masks considerable variation. DHHS-ACF has tabulated the caseload decline from January 1993 to June 2000, deriving a federal caseload decline for California of 42 percent.[8] The state with the second largest caseload, New York, also had a decline of 42 percent. Only six states had smaller declines.

---

[8]Note that these are not the ALF-202 caseload figures used to compute the caseload reduction credit (discussed in Section 2). Those caseload figures add back in the SSP cases.

However, this comparison overstates the total caseload decline in California. The published DHHS caseload counts consider only the federal caseload. Thus, they reflect the removal of two-parent cases in states (including California) that established SSPs for two-parent cases near the end of this period. Adding the two-parent caseload back in brings the state's caseload decline over this period (January 1993 to June 2000) to about 34 percent. Only three states had smaller declines, and several states had much larger declines.

Finally, the percentage increase in California's population was slightly larger than that for the nation. Thus, about 4 percentage points of the slower decrease in the caseload in California results from the state's faster population growth. However, a large differential remains.

Possible Explanations for the Descriptive Findings

This review of caseload trends suggests two complementary sets of questions. The first set includes the following: Why did California's caseload decline? In particular, what was the role of CalWORKs in the caseload decline? Of state-level policies? Of CWD programs?

The second set includes the following: Why was California's caseload decline smaller than the decline in the rest of the nation? Why did California's caseload decline begin later? In particular, what was the role of differences in policies and programs between CalWORKs and other TANF programs in the differential caseload decline?

In this subsection, we use the model and factors described in Section 1 (Figure 1.1) to identify possible answers to these two sets of questions.

What Might Explain the Magnitude and Timing of the Caseload Decline in California?

California's caseload decline is driven mostly by the economy, some by pre-CalWORKs reforms, some by other policies, and some by county CalWORKs programs.

The Effect of the Economy. The economy is a natural candidate for explaining much of the caseload decline. Few would argue that the increase in the caseload in the early 1990s was the result of a massive collapse of casework or policies that became more generous. It seems likely that much of the caseload increase was the result of the worsening economy during that period. This inference is supported by the simple co-movement of the unemployment rate (as a proxy for

44

economic conditions) and the economy, plotted in Figure 3.4. Like the caseload, the unemployment rate rises in the early 1990s and falls in the late 1990s. While the unemployment rate appears to lead the caseload by about two years, the turning points for the underlying flows of the caseload—discussed in more detail below—are very close to those for the economy. The lag in the relation between the unemployment rate and the caseload derives from the way changes in the flows affect changes in the total caseload.

Similarly, the differential paths of the caseload by region are consistent with differential unemployment-rate paths by region. For both the unemployment rate and the caseload, the largest increases and subsequent declines are in Southern California. There is a small increase and then a large decline in the Bay Area, and smaller changes both up and down in the Central Valley and Northern California.

From its peak in March 1993, the unemployment rate fell nearly continuously through the summer of 2000. Thus, just as economic conditions explained some of the increase in the caseload, they appear to explain some of the decline in the

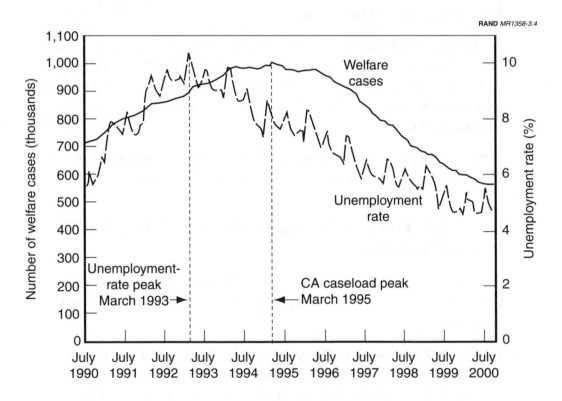

Figure 3.4—California's Unemployment Rate and Welfare Caseload

caseload well past the passage and implementation of CalWORKs. In addition, given the lag in the relation between the economy and the caseload, the unemployment-rate declines through the summer of 2000 seem likely to pull down the caseload well into 2001.

The Effect of Pre-CalWORKs Reforms. The existing WTW programs are not a likely explanation for the pre-CalWORKs caseload patterns. California's WTW programs were relatively stable and employment-and-training-focused until the 1995 GAIN reforms. Furthermore, most of those reforms were apparently not implemented even on the eve of CalWORKs. (The exceptions appear to have been Riverside County, Monterey County, Santa Barbara County, San Mateo County, and Sonoma County.)

There were, however, two major reforms to California welfare programs in the early 1990s. In response to the state's fiscal crisis, the nominal aid payment was cut several times (see Appendix A). In addition, the COLA was suspended. The combination of the cuts in the nominal benefit, the suspension of the COLA, and the moderate inflation rate during the early part of the period combined to yield a nearly 29 percent cut in the real welfare payment between 1991 and 1997. Conventional estimates (e.g., Council of Economic Advisers, 1999; Blank, 2001) imply that this 29 percent cut would have been expected to lower the caseload by 7 to 16 percent.

In addition, in 1992, California adopted fill-the-gap budgeting and in 1993, California implemented the Work Pays reforms. As discussed in Section 2, these reforms made work more attractive for those currently on welfare, increasing the level of earnings at which a recipient becomes income-ineligible for cash assistance (the breakeven point). This enabled some people whose earnings would previously have made them income-ineligible for welfare to remain on the welfare rolls, in turn increasing the caseload. Such an increase in the caseload has been found in similar benefit-structure reforms in other states (see, e.g., Berlin, 2000). We note, however, that the random assignment of the California Work Pays reforms produced few statistically significant or substantively large effects. Meyers, Glaser, and MacDonald (1998) conclude that part of the problem was that recipients were not informed of the changes in the benefit structure. Not knowing that the incentives had changed, they did not change their behavior. In response to these findings, CDSS moved to increase awareness of the changes, but no evaluation of this campaign is available.

The Effect of Other Government Policies. Other government policy changes are also likely to have affected the caseload in the early 1990s. Large increases in the EITC made work more attractive relative to welfare (Hotz and Scholz, 2000;

Meyer and Rosenbaum, 1999, 2000) and thus would have been expected to decrease the caseload.

Conversely, immigration reform would have been expected to decrease the caseload in the late 1980s and then increase it in the early 1990s. In particular, those legalized through IRCA were subject to the five-year moratorium on welfare receipt. When that period ended in late 1993 and 1994, an influx of new cases would have been expected, especially among Hispanics and especially in Los Angeles County, Southern California, and the Central Valley. The race/ethnicity and regional patterns are consistent with this presumption. (See MaCurdy, Mancuso, and O'Brien-Strain (2000) for further evidence on the effects of IRCA.)

The Effect of County Welfare Programs. A simple timing argument allows us to bound the effects of CalWORKs on the caseload decline. California's caseload peaked in March 1995. The turning points in the flows—rates of entry into welfare and rates of exit from welfare—occurred more than a year earlier. Federal welfare reform, PRWORA, did not pass until August 1996; CalWORKs did not pass until August 1997; and one-on-one casework reflecting the new CalWORKs WTW programs did not begin in volume until the summer of 1998, with many components following a year or more later. Thus, we would not expect the main impact of expanded and reformed county welfare programs on the caseload until early 1999. In fact, Figure 3.5 provides some evidence of such effects in this time frame. The figure presents the caseload from a dynamic perspective.[9] The line labeled *Net change* plots the monthly percentage change in the caseload. It is positive where the caseload is growing (through early 1995) and then turns negative as the caseload shrinks.

Figure 3.5 also plots the entry rate (per capita x 10). To adjust the scale, the entries are multiplied by ten. This series peaks in mid-1991 (at about 0.41 percent), staying more or less at that level through mid-1993. Only then does it begin its rapid fall, to about 0.2 percent in late 1998. It has risen slightly since then, but not as fast as the entry rate as a percentage of the caseload. Thus, the upturn in the entry rate per case appears to result primarily from the continuing fall in the caseload rather than from an increase in the rate of entry among those off welfare.

Finally, Figure 3.5 plots the exit rate per case. As expected, exits move in the opposite direction from entrances (per capita, at least until 1999). When

---

[9]These estimates are computed from MEDS data. To smooth out seasonal variation, the plots are the one-year moving average of the monthly rates.

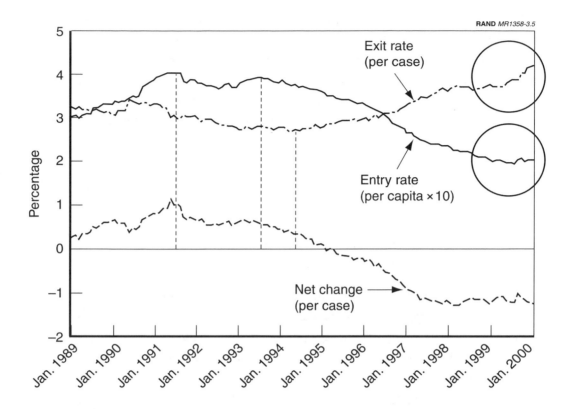

SOURCE: RAND tabulations from 5 percent MEDS mircrodata.

Figure 3.5—Changes in Flows Onto and Off Welfare

entrances rise, exits fall; when entrances fall, exits rise. Exits as a percentage of the caseload reached their lowest point in mid-1994, at about 2.7 percent. Thereafter, they have risen rapidly and nearly continuously, to over 4.1 percent by 2000.

These patterns are broadly consistent with the patterns for the caseload: A worsening in the early 1990s, followed by robust and sustained improvement in the late 1990s. Note, however, that the turning points in the flows are earlier. The total caseload begins to decline in about March 1995. Entrances per capita peak in mid-1991, but the sustained decline does not begin until mid-1993. Exits per case begin to increase about mid-1994. These turning points are a year or two before the turning point in the caseload but nearly simultaneous with the turning point in the state's economy.

Returning to the question of the effect of county welfare programs on the decline of the caseload, the circled areas in Figure 3.5 show that toward the end of the available data, the entrance rate per capita had stopped falling, which would be

48

expected to stop the exit rate from rising. In fact, however, the exit rate has continued to rise. County WTW programs that primarily affect the caseload by helping current recipients leave faster are one possible explanation for the divergence of the trends between entrances and exits. Evidence on employment since entering welfare, which is presented in the next section, is also consistent with an important role for county WTW programs in decreasing the caseload in the most recent period.

What Might Explain the Smaller Caseload Decline in California Compared with the Rest of the Nation?

The economy and different statewide policies account for the lower caseload decline in California versus the rest of the nation.

The Effect of the Economy. Just as the path of the unemployment rate in California explains part of the increase in California's caseload, it seems likely that the path of the national unemployment rate explains part of the path of the national caseload. Figure 3.6 shows that, like the unemployment rate in

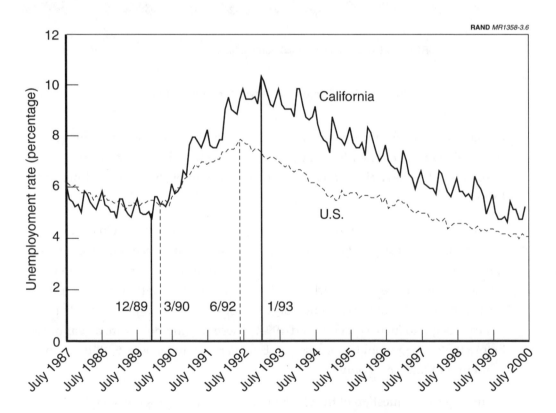

Figure 3.6—Unemployment Rates for California and the Nation

California, the national unemployment rate rose in the early 1990s and has fallen since then. Furthermore, the rise in the unemployment rate in California was sharper and the peak occurred later. This pattern—larger increase and later peak—is similar to the relative caseload paths between California and the nation.

These inferences from aggregate time series are also supported by econometric (double-fixed effects) analyses (Council of Economic Advisers, 1997, 1999; Figlio and Ziliak, 1999), which conclude that the economy is the largest single factor explaining the differential paths of the caseload across states. There is some disagreement in the literature about the importance of the economy in explaining the caseload decline. Based on their dynamic approach, Klerman and Haider (2001) argue that the largest estimates (i.e., Figlio and Ziliak's dynamic models) are too large, but estimates from the widely cited CEA estimates are probably too small. Most studies conclude that the economy is more important in explaining the early decline (up to and possibly slightly past PRWORA) and less important in the later period (as state TANF programs were implemented and policies and programs diverged).

Thus, the available evidence suggests that some of California's larger caseload increase and later and smaller caseload decline were caused by the economy. However, once it started, California's recovery (i.e., the decline in the unemployment rate) was faster than that of the nation as a whole. Thus, inasmuch as changes in the unemployment rate cause changes in the caseload (or the flows), the economy should have caused the decline in California's caseload (perhaps a lag of a year or two) to be larger than in the other states (which it was not).

The Effect of CalWORKs Legislation. Nationally, waiver-enabled changes to state welfare programs accelerated in the years immediately preceding PRWORA. Increasing numbers of states strengthened their participation requirements, raised their sanctions for nonparticipation (first adopting any sanction, then adopting a full-family sanction), and imposed lifetime time limits.

These changes continued to accelerate after PRWORA, as states exploited their new discretion to design their own TANF programs. Most states adopted a full-family sanction and ended aid for the entire family at the time limit. Many states adopted a shorter time limit.

California also adopted changes to its welfare program with TANF. Thus, as TANF policy changes decreased the national caseload (and the evidence is that it did—see Council of Economic Advisers, 1997, 1999), we would expect the CalWORKs policy changes to decrease California's caseload. Indeed, both the national evidence (e.g., Council of Economic Advisers, 1997, 1999) and the

California evidence (e.g., Klerman and Haider, 2001) suggest that much of the caseload decline is not explained by the economy.

Policy effects can be expected to occur primarily after the policies are implemented. The new benefit structure and time-limit clocks were not implemented until January 1998. The new participation requirements would not be expected to affect caseloads until county programs ramped up—at the earliest, in the summer and fall of 1998; for other purposes, in 1999 and into 2000.

Nevertheless, it seems plausible that some effects of reforms preceded the implementation of the programs. In many counties, with the passage of PRWORA in the summer of 1996, caseworkers started to explain to recipients that the old world of time-unlimited welfare was ending, that the economy was good, and that now was a good time to leave aid. The evidence from national studies (e.g., Levine and Whitmore, 1998; Blank, 2001) suggests that caseload declines often lead the actual implementation of reforms.

Compared to the TANF changes in other states, however, CalWORKs represented less of a change relative to AFDC/GAIN. Since these policy changes were smaller in California, we would expect the caseload effects also to be smaller (and to occur later) in California.

Precisely which of the policies has had the largest effect is the subject of considerable ongoing debate (Council of Economic Advisers, 1997, 1999; Rector and Youssef, 1999; Ellwood, 1999). Because states adopted the policies as bundles in the midst of a robust economic expansion, it is difficult to estimate the individual effects of those policies. Here, we briefly discuss the evidence for three clusters of policy changes: benefit structure, participation requirements and sanctions, and time limits.

Benefit Structure. As noted earlier, California has among the highest benefit levels in the country, as well as a high earned-income disregard and a low BRR. Thus, the earnings at which welfare recipients become income-ineligible for benefits are among the very highest in the country. Our simulation results (discussed in Section 2 and illustrated in Appendix D) imply that California's caseload would be about 9 percent smaller if the state adopted the benefit structure of other states.

Yet it seems unlikely that benefit structure alone explains either the large caseload decline in California or the smaller caseload decline in California relative to that of the nation as a whole. The 1993 Work Pays reforms and the extensions to those reforms in the 1997 CalWORKs legislation would have been expected to raise the caseload (at least in the short run), since individuals who would have become income-ineligible under the earlier benefit structure remained eligible.

Similarly, the CalWORKs changes to the benefit structure are unlikely to explain California's smaller caseload decline. It is true that CalWORKs further increased the income-ineligibility level, which would be expected to increase the caseload; however, our simulations based on Q5 data suggest that there are relatively few people with earnings between the pre-CalWORKs and post-CalWORKs income-eligibility levels, so the net effect was to increase the caseload by only about 2 percent.[10]

The effects in other states were larger. Work Pays-type reforms were common components of state TANF programs.[11] Other states started with lower benefit levels, lower earnings disregards, and higher BRRs. Thus, the increase in the income-ineligibility level included a larger fraction of potential recipients, increasing the caseload in other states even more than the CalWORKs changes did in California. The simulations suggest that the smaller benefit-structure reforms in California would have narrowed the gap between California's caseload and that of the nation as a whole by about 2 percentage points.

Work Requirements and Sanctions. By contrast, it seems likely that the combination of participation requirements and sanction policies does explain some (perhaps much) of the differential caseload decline. With pre-PRWORA waivers and then redesigned TANF programs, states moved aggressively to link receipt of cash assistance to work and to penalize those who did not participate.[12]

Many states require pre-approval job search, often including some form of Job Club. Once on aid, recipients are expected to participate in WTW activities. In some of the states with the largest caseload decline, the goal is "complete engagement"—every recipient participating in some activity every day. Leaders in those states report that once informed of the requirement for pre-approval job search and post-approval participation, some recipients choose not to complete the application and some current recipients leave. (In California, some counties report similar outcomes after the imposition of the community service requirement.)

---

[10]This estimate is computed using methods similar to those used to produce Table D.1, which include the behavioral response. However, if there are fixed costs to being on welfare so that individuals eligible for small checks choose to leave, this estimate is likely to be too low.

[11]According to Bloom and Pavetti (2001), 40 states adopted such reforms.

[12]See Gais et al. (2001) on linking aid to work and the role of pre-approval job search.

For those who remain on welfare but do not participate, most states have streamlined their conciliation process—first under waivers and then in their TANF programs. This streamlining of the conciliation process in other states has led advocates in those states to express concern that many people are being sanctioned inappropriately—that they were not given a chance to show good cause, they did not know that they were noncompliant, and notices were not received or were difficult to interpret (see, e.g., Overby, 1998; U.S. Department of Health and Human Services, 1998; Goldberg and Schott, 2000).

The magnitude of the sanction has also changed. In 37 states, the entire benefit is eliminated (a full-family sanction) rather than only the adult part, either at the first noncompliance event (in 15 states) or at some subsequent event (in 22 states). In seven states, continued or repeated noncompliance can lead to a lifetime bar on receipt of welfare (Goldberg and Schott, 2000; Bloom and Pavetti, 2001). Goldberg and Schott (2000) estimate that about one-third of case closures result from sanctions.

Bloom and Pavetti (2001) conclude that these policies are important in explaining the observed caseload decline. Some applicants or recipients choose to leave welfare (or not to apply) rather than participate. Some participate and find jobs through the WTW services provided. With the lower benefit structure in many other states, employment for enough hours to satisfy the participation rate requirement is enough to make them income-ineligible. Finally, those who choose not to comply are sanctioned. With a full-family sanction, they are dropped from the caseload.

A large number of cases appear to be dropped because of full-family sanctions. The Council of Economic Advisers (1999) estimated that a full-family sanction cuts the welfare caseload by more than 10 percent. Goldberg and Schott (2000) estimated that at the end of 1999, 370,000 cases nationally had received a full-family sanction and remained off welfare. This is 15 percent of the national caseload. Furthermore, the effects are concentrated in the states with full-family sanctions (most of the states, but only about half of the national caseload). In seven states, one-fifth or more of the case closures resulted from full-family sanctions.

The situation in California is quite different. Since the mid-1980s, California had had a mandatory WTW program with moderate levels of adult-only sanctions, so the adoption of the program in the early 1990s did not cause any caseload decline (see, e.g., Council of Economic Advisers, 1997, 1999). Inasmuch as WTW programs help recipients get jobs, the benefit structure implies that recipients remain eligible for cash assistance and often still receive aid.

In addition, the CalWORKs statute specifically prohibits requiring pre-approval job search (though voluntary pre-approval job search is legal). CWDs report that many recipients in California do not attend appraisal or complete Job Club. In many other states, job search is required before the case is opened, so the welfare case of such people (who do not complete job search) would not have been opened.

Furthermore, while CalWORKs includes a universal participation requirement, the requirement is not enforced as a complete engagement program, at least not until community service. The details of the regulations imply that even compliant recipients are unlikely to reach mandatory community service until after about 30 months of continuous receipt of cash assistance (six or more months until they sign a WTW plan plus 18 or 24 months of WTW activities after signing a plan). For those who exit and reenter or who are noncompliant, mandatory community service comes even later. Counties were still filing their community service plans, setting up their community service programs, and enrolling recipients in volume in the fall of 2000—two and a half years after CalWORKs was enacted. Consistent with the reports of other states, some counties report that when faced with mandatory community service, a sizable fraction of recipients do something else: they find a job, become noncompliant, or leave cash assistance. However, very few recipients have reached the community service point.

Similarly with respect to sanction policy, CalWORKs retained the GAIN noncompliance process—a multistep conciliation process and then an adults-only sanction. The evaluation's fieldwork and staff survey suggest that caseworkers, often with the strong encouragement of CWD leadership, give recipients multiple opportunities to comply before even beginning the formal noncompliance process. Caseworkers note that some recipients take advantage of the noncompliance process itself to delay the start of formal noncompliance proceedings and then the sanction.

Nevertheless, about 11 percent of the adults in one-parent cases are in sanction and another 8 percent are formally noncompliant but not yet sanctioned. In addition, it appears that some of those not participating are noncompliant but not yet in the formal noncompliance system. The total number of adults who have at some point in their time on aid become noncompliant appears to be much larger.

The GAO (2000) presents evidence that some (perhaps half) of these adults would come into compliance with a more quickly and surely applied full-family sanction, but some of them would not.[13] In a full-family sanction state, such noncompliant cases would be dropped from the caseload. It seems likely that a strictly applied full-family sanction would cut California's caseload by more than 10 percentage points (Council of Economic Advisers, 1999).

Time Limits. The major program innovation of the immediate pre-PRWORA period was lifetime time limits on welfare receipt. First implemented in Florida and Connecticut, these programs became the defining element of the PRWORA reforms. They are embedded in the name of the new program—Temporary Assistance for Needy Families. Furthermore, instead of giving states more discretion on time limits, PRWORA includes a national ban on the use of federal funds to pay cash assistance to adults past the federal 60-month time limit.

Following the direction provided by the federal legislation, almost all states have adopted lifetime time limits.[14] In 43 states (including the District of Columbia), after reaching the time limit, the entire case may be terminated; however, in practice, a sizable fraction of those reaching time limits receive (often short) extensions. Furthermore, in 17 states that account for one-quarter of the national caseload, a case reaches the time limit in fewer than 60 months (Bloom and Pavetti, 2001).

In contrast, California has adopted among the least binding time-limit policies. Recipients receive the full 60 months; the start date for the 60-month clock is among the latest in the country, January 1998; and after the time limit is reached, payments to the children continue. Thus, inasmuch as time limits would be expected to decrease the caseload—either because recipients leave to preserve or "bank" their months of eligibility or because they reach time limits—those caseload effects should be smaller in California.

The magnitude of the effect of time limits on the caseload is the subject of some controversy. At least until recently, few recipients actually reached time limits. Apparently, even in states where recipients could already have done so, few did. The strong economy and strong sanctions imply that recipients find jobs (and benefits in many states are so low that once recipients find jobs, they are income-ineligible and leave welfare), or they become noncompliant and a full-family sanction terminates their cases.

---

[13]In Iowa, half of those sanctioned come back into compliance; in other states, 30 percent come back. This estimate does not include the deterrent effect, i.e., it does not include those who participate because of the threat of a full-family sanction.

[14]A few states (e.g., Michigan, Vermont, and New York) adopted no time limit, choosing instead to fund past the federal limit out of state funds.

Consistent with these conclusions, MDRC's random-assignment studies of the early experiences in Florida and Connecticut found that most recipients leave before reaching the time limits. Furthermore, those randomly assigned to the time-limit group were no more likely to leave before reaching the time limit, i.e., they did not appear to bank their months (Bloom et al., 2000; Fein and Karweit, 1997; Gordon and Agodini, 1999).

Grogger and Michalopoulos (1999) and Grogger (2000) dispute these conclusions. They note that time limits were usually adopted in a bundle along with Work Pays-type policies. The Work Pays-type policies would have been expected to increase the caseload, counteracting any expected effect of banking. In addition, these authors note that in some states, those in the time-limit group did not realize that they were subject to time limits, while many of those not in the time-limit group thought they were subject to time limits. Finally, they present econometric evidence suggesting moderate effects of time limits (about 6 percentage points).

Our simulations imply that California's time-limit policies have increased the caseload relative to what it would have been if California had adopted the time-limit policies of other states.[15] As of mid-2000, the leading edge of recipients have reached time limits in about one-third of the states, including Texas, Florida, and North Carolina. About 10 percent of California's caseload is already past the time limit of the "average" state. According to each state's exemption policy, some of these cases would have been terminated. If, as Grogger argues, recipients leave cash assistance to bank their eligibility, then the effect of California's 60-month time limit would be even larger than is implied by the simulation.

Over the next year and a half, the relative effect of time limits on caseload is likely to increase. In most states that adopted 60-month time limits, the first cases will reach those limits in late 2001 or early 2002. In states with termination time limits, these cases will disappear, causing the caseload to drop sharply. In California, the first cases will not reach time limits until January 2003. Even then, only the adults' benefits will be terminated. Thus, the direct effect on the caseload will be small.

---

[15]The simulation considers the effect separately for each state's sanction policy. The national effect is estimated by averaging over all of the states, weighting by each state's caseload.

4. Outcomes for Leavers

Federal welfare reform fundamentally shifted the focus of welfare policy from providing cash assistance to those currently on welfare to providing temporary assistance. However, the goal of the program is not merely to cut the welfare rolls; it is also to end the dependence of needy parents on government assistance. Thus, we are interested in the status of those who leave the welfare system (referred to here as "leavers").

This section considers the experiences of leavers, starting with an overview of the descriptive findings. We next examine the support for those findings, starting with a consideration of the extent to which leavers stay leavers, i.e., rates of return to welfare. Employment, earnings, and earnings growth are then examined, first by time since leaving welfare, and then by time since entering welfare, whether they remain on welfare or leave. We argue that in the post-TANF era, the second measure is probably more appropriate for considering the performance of county WTW programs. We then consider take-up of Medi-Cal among welfare leavers. Finally, we look at outcomes, not only for welfare leavers but for all single-mother households. After presenting the specific descriptive findings, we conclude with a discussion of the likely causes of the observed changes and the implications of the findings for WTW programs and the well-being of welfare leavers.

Overview of Descriptive Findings

The rapid caseload decline (discussed in Section 3) suggests a concern that county CalWORKs programs might be pushing households off welfare before they are ready. This would result in outcomes for leavers in the post-CalWORKs period being significantly worse than they had been pre-CalWORKs. In fact, almost all the indicators improve under CalWORKs, through the most recent data. Rates of return are down, and employment and earnings are up, as is Medi-Cal enrollment. Among entrants, rates of leaving are up and so are employment and earnings. Among all single-parent families, employment and earnings are up and poverty is down.

Return to Welfare

We begin our consideration of outcomes for welfare leavers by asking how frequently leavers return to cash assistance. Figure 4.1 shows how return to cash assistance varies with time since receipt of such assistance and calendar time.

"Leaving" is defined as being off cash assistance for all three months of a calendar quarter.[1] The last quarter on welfare is quarter 0; by construction, all leavers are off welfare in quarter 1; by quarter 2, some recipients are back. Figure 4.1 shows outcomes through 12 quarters (i.e., three years) after leaving welfare,

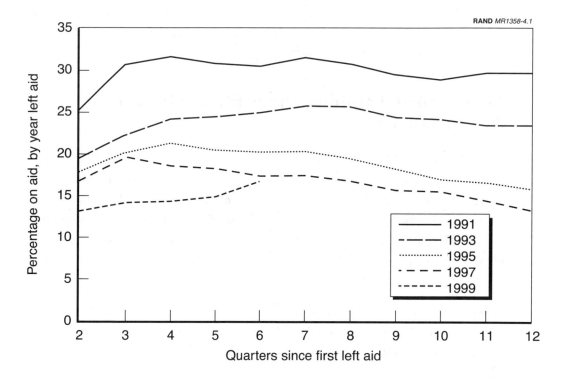

SOURCE: RAND tabulations from 5 percent MEDS-EDD microdata match file.

Figure 4.1—Return to Welfare

---

[1]Leavers are defined as persons off aid for at least two consecutive months; they remain in our sample even if they subsequently return to aid. We study leavers 18 to 64 years of age, for whom up to one Social Security number matched from EDD data. Our EDD data range from 1990 Q3 to 2000 Q2, so the sample sizes for the 1990 and 2000 cohorts are smaller than for other years, and the estimates are less precise.

While we know which months individuals were on or off aid, we know only total quarterly earnings. Thus, we cannot discern which months of the quarter someone worked, so in our analyses, we drop these "transition" quarters.

including second and later exits from welfare. Each line on the chart refers to a cohort of leavers (i.e., those last on aid in a given calendar year).

The figure suggests that exit from welfare is not always permanent. Of those leaving welfare in 1997, about 15 percent were back on welfare in the second quarter. In quarters three through eight, more leavers returned, but some of the leavers exited a second time. In net, the number of leavers who are back on welfare each quarter remains approximately constant at about 15 percent.

Figure 4.1 also suggests that over the period covered by the data, rates of return to welfare decreased sharply. In the early 1990s, one-fourth or more of welfare recipients were back on welfare by the second quarter, and the fraction rose with quarters since leaving aid. Rates of return fell sharply and steadily through the mid-1990s, so that by 1999, they were below 20 percent.

Employment, Earnings, and Earnings Growth Among Leavers

The CalWORKs legislation envisions exits to aid through employment. First, the Work Pays reforms and their CalWORKs extensions encourage recipients to build labor-market experience while on welfare. Second, Job Club is intended to give recipients skills to find jobs. Third, education and training are intended to build skills that will allow recipients to find jobs or advance to better jobs. Finally, job-retention services are intended to help recipients keep the jobs they have and advance to better ones.

In this subsection, we examine how leavers are faring in terms of any kind of employment and earnings growth and in terms of full-time employment; finally, using the trends in these areas, we discuss how leavers are supporting themselves.

How Welfare Leavers Are Faring in Terms of Any Employment and Earnings Growth

We have already seen in Section 2 that the fraction of *current recipients* working and the fraction of recipients earning more than cut-off values have increased sharply and steadily since about 1993.[2] Figure 4.2 presents the employment rates of welfare leavers, and the story is similar.

---

[2]We show only data from odd-numbered years to simplify the figures; trends in even-numbered years follow the same pattern, adding little information.

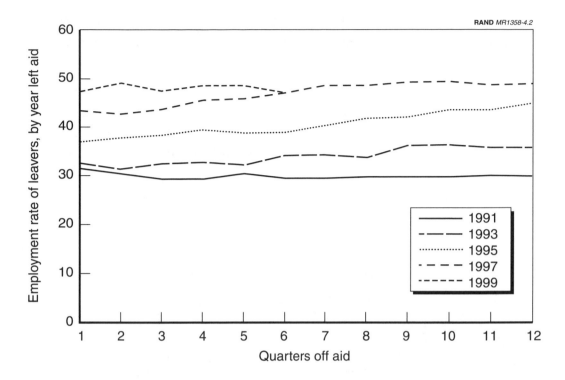

SOURCE: RAND tabulations from 5 percent MEDS-EDD microdata match file.

Figure 4.2—Employment of Leavers per Quarter by Year of Exit and Quarters Since Exit

The structure of the figure is similar to that of Figure 4.1. Each line shows the percentage of all leavers (those leaving in a calendar year) who have any earnings of over $50 per quarter, by quarters since leaving welfare. The estimates are computed based on the same underlying UI system filings used in Section 2. Thus, any earnings in a calendar quarter not covered by the UI system (e.g., earnings from self-employment and independent contracting) are excluded from the calculations. This means that these estimates are a lower bound on the true levels of employment.[3] Leavers remain in the estimates even if they return to cash assistance.

The implications of Figure 4.2 are also similar to those of Figure 4.1. In the most recent cohorts (leavers in 1999 and 2000), employment rates hover at about 50 percent—half of the leavers are employed, and this fraction is stable with time since leaving welfare. This level of employment represents a significant increase over earlier cohorts of leavers. For the cohort leaving welfare in 1993,

---

[3]Evidence from surveys and other studies suggests that true levels of employment are roughly seven percentage points higher than those recorded in UI data. The Statewide CalWORKs Evaluation's household survey provides California-specific evidence on this issue.

employment levels hovered at about 30 percent, much lower than today's 50 percent levels. Rates of employment increased steadily through the 1994, 1995, and 1996 cohorts, after which they leveled off at approximately 50 percent.

While employment is an important outcome in and of itself, the goal of CalWORKs is self-sufficiency, so earnings (and their growth) are of equal significance. Figure 4.3 presents the level of real earnings per quarter among leavers (in year 2000 dollars).[4] All leavers are included in the calculations,

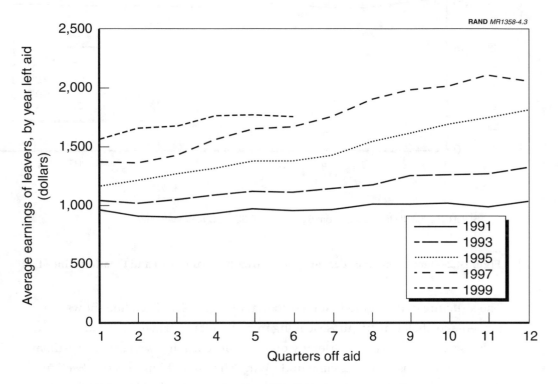

SOURCE: RAND tabulations from 5 percent MEDS-EDD microdata match file.

Figure 4.3—Average Quarterly Earnings of Leavers

_____

[4]Earnings are deflated using the national Consumer Price Index-Urban Consumers (CPI-U); the monthly values are averaged to calculate a quarterly CPI. Employers are required by EDD only to report earnings of employees who earn more than $50 in a quarter, though some employers report earnings for all workers. Because the records are incomplete for workers earning less than $50 in a quarter, we reassign workers with such low earnings whose employers happened to report them to EDD to the nonwork category to maintain consistency.

We also ignore transition quarters, i.e., the quarters in which someone was both on aid and off aid, because while we know exactly which months someone was on aid, we do not know which months they worked. The distinction is especially important for entrants, since we cannot determine if they left a job and started on aid or were unemployed, went on aid, and found a job through the welfare department. Similarly, we cannot tell if leavers found work through their CWDs, left aid and then lost their jobs, or left aid and then found work.

whether they stay off welfare or return to welfare, and whether or not they are employed.

Like the trends in Figure 4.1 and Figure 4.2, real earnings among welfare leavers are higher for later cohorts of leavers. Average earnings of the 1993 cohort in the quarter after leaving welfare were just over $1,000 (in year 2000 dollars); average earnings of the cohorts from 1998 forward in the quarter after leaving welfare are about 50 percent higher (about $1,500).

Furthermore, earnings rise about 10 percent in each of the first three years after leaving welfare.[5] This estimate is consistent with recent national estimates of wage growth for welfare leavers (Gladden and Taber, 2000; Corcoran and Loeb, 1999). However, it is important to note that at least on average, the earnings growth is from a very low base (i.e., only about one-fourth of the sample have earnings equivalent to full-time work at the minimum wage).

How Leavers Are Faring in Terms of Full-Time Work and Household Resources

This average earnings measure mixes very different groups—some who have no earnings, some who work part-time, some who work full-time at low wages, and some who work full-time at a wage considerably above the minimum wage. The relative size of the different groups is important. A family of three does not become income-ineligible for cash assistance until earnings reach the equivalent of full-time work at about $8.75 an hour. Furthermore, the federal EITC is designed so that even at the lower federal minimum wage, $5.15, a family of four with one full-time worker would be out of poverty. For welfare leavers, these computations traditionally consider a family of three. For that case, full-time work at California's minimum wage (as of January 2001) of $6.25, when combined with the federal EITC and Food Stamps, gives a household cash and near-cash (i.e., Food Stamps) resources about 25 percent above the poverty level.[6]

Some have argued that the official poverty level is too low. However, when in-kind benefits—child care, Medi-Cal, and transportation—are included, the value of the package exceeds the California Budget Project's (1999) estimate of what it

---

[5] The increase discussed in the text is for average reported earnings. It does not refer to any individual. Earnings could rise because a leaver's wages rise, or because hours for an already working leaver rise, or because formerly nonworking leavers begin to work.

[6] This computation cashes out the value of public assistance and Food Stamps, while the conventional definition of the poverty line does not. See Haskins, Sawhill, and Weaver (2001) for a similar calculation.

costs to "raise a family in California."[7] Thus, if a leaver works at or near full-time and uses all of the available benefits (in fact, however, take-up appears to be far from universal), even at the minimum wage, her family will be out of poverty.

However, the data suggest that few leavers are reaching that level of income. The EDD data do not include information on hours. However, we can create a proxy for hours by assuming employment at the minimum wage (for these calculations, $5.75).[8] Using this proxy, Figure 4.4 plots the proportion of leavers who have EDD earnings equivalent to full-time work at the minimum wage. The figure shows that the fraction of leavers working the equivalent of full-time at the minimum wage has risen dramatically, but the levels remain low. In the early 1990s, only about 15 percent of leavers had earnings at this level. By the most

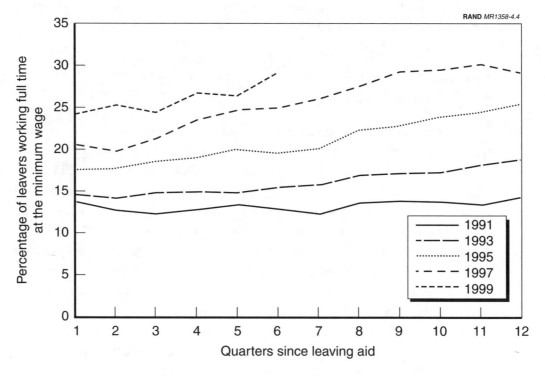

SOURCE: RAND tabulations from 5 percent MEDS-EDD microdata match file.

Figure 4.4—Percentage of Leavers with Quarterly Earnings Greater Than Full-Time Work at Minimum Wage by Calendar Year and Time Since Leaving Welfare

---

[7]See Appendix C for details.

[8]Here we use this real $5.75 level in each year. Given inflation and changes in the nominal value of the minimum wage, this computation does not reflect hours at the then-statutory minimum wage.

recent cohorts, the fraction had risen to about 25 percent. Furthermore, the fraction rises to about 30 percent in three years. Nevertheless, these absolute levels of full-time equivalent work appear low. (This may be explained partly by incomplete coverage of earnings by the UI system on which these tabulations are based.)

Finally, this basic story—a rising fraction of leavers working the equivalent of full-time at the minimum wage, but low absolute levels—is not sensitive to the hours cutoff chosen. Some have argued that single mothers should not be expected to work full-time. PRWORA defines participation as 25 hours per week; CalWORKs adopts a higher level, 32 hours per week. Nevertheless, when we repeat this analysis for 20 or 25 hours per week, the fraction of leavers with earnings above the threshold increases, but the general pattern remains.

Only 24 percent of those leaving welfare in 1999 have earnings (in the EDD data) greater than the equivalent of full-time (40 hours) work at the minimum wage. Lowering the cutoff to the 32-hours-per-week standard in the CalWORKs legislation raises the figure to 28 percent; lowering the cutoff to the 25-hours-per week standard in the federal legislation raises the figure to 32 percent. Furthermore, there is some evidence of an increase over time in the fraction of leavers earning more than the cutoff. Nevertheless, at least from the EDD data, a clear majority appear not to be working even 25 hours per week.

Given Employment Levels, How Are Leavers Supporting Themselves?

The analyses in this section clearly show that labor-market outcomes are improving. Employment, average earnings, and the fraction of leavers earning more than the equivalent of full-time at the minimum wage are rising rapidly.

Despite these strong trends, only about one-half of all welfare leavers are working, and only about one-quarter are working full-time. If they are neither receiving welfare nor working, how are they supporting themselves and their children?

This question is not unique to California. National studies find that one-third to one-half of welfare leavers have no reported earnings (Parrott, 1998; Brauner and Loprest, 1999).

Some of the reported nonemployment and low earnings is probably real. National data suggest that some welfare leavers are receiving support from others—spouses, nonmarital partners, parents, other relatives, friends—and some are receiving support from other government programs. One possibility is SSI, but that appears to be received in less than 5 percent of the households of leavers.

Finally, some of the reported nonemployment is probably a reporting issue. The results reported here are based on employer UI system filings to the EDD, where only employment in the state of California is recorded. Earnings from non-California employers (including those who have moved out of state) are not recorded.[9] Furthermore, self-employment (including independent contracting) and federal government employment are not covered by the UI system and are therefore not reported to EDD. Finally, no "under-the-table" income is reported to EDD. National data from surveys suggest that the group includes about 7 percent of those with no income (ASPE, 2000; Cancian et al., 1999).

Examining the low absolute levels of employment and earnings and, in particular, the relative importance of income not reported to EDD and support from others is one of our tasks for the coming year. We are currently cross-checking information from several sources—EDD records, the evaluation's household survey, and other government records—to explore these issues further. No data source provides complete coverage of earnings; by cross-checking the various surveys and reviewing the results of similar efforts in other states, we should be able to develop a better sense of how to interpret the EDD data and the evidence as a whole.

Entering Cohorts versus Leaving Cohorts

Our discussion thus far has, like conventional "leavers studies" (e.g., Loprest, 1999), focused on leavers alone. (We discussed outcomes for current recipients separately in Section 2.) However, this approach is arguably not fully consistent with TANF's focus on converting current recipients into leavers, i.e., providing only temporary assistance.

In particular, if WTW programs succeed in moving the most work-ready recipients into the labor force and off aid, employment and earnings levels might fall for those on aid (and perhaps for those off aid as well). Tabulated employment and earnings levels might fall for current recipients because the most work-ready have left aid.[10] Nevertheless, even if this occurred, we could

---

[9]Kornfeld and Bloom (1999) claim that this is not significant.

[10]Tabulated employment and earnings levels for leavers might fall because the leavers, though job-ready, may not find as good jobs as did those who left in previous periods (without program intervention).

still consider the program a success; new entrants get jobs faster and at higher earnings, and they leave welfare faster.

In addition to tabulating results separately for current recipients and leavers, it may be useful to perform complementary analyses of outcomes since entering welfare, regardless of whether the leavers are currently receiving welfare. How long does it take until a new recipient finds a first job, regardless of welfare receipt? What are average earnings, regardless of welfare receipt? This perspective is arguably more useful for evaluating program effects. Figures 4.5 and 4.6 provide that perspective. Corresponding to Figures 4.2 and 4.3, they plot employment and average earnings by quarters since first *entering* welfare.

As expected, the levels of work and earnings are lower for entrants than for leavers, but the trends are similar. Later cohorts of entrants into welfare are moving into jobs faster and have higher earnings. In particular, rates of employment and average earnings are much higher for the early post-CalWORKs cohorts (entrants in 1998 and 1999). In fact, in the most recent cohorts, employment levels and average earnings are sometimes lower for recent

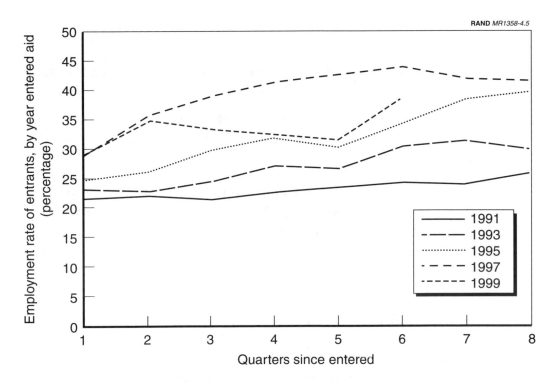

SOURCE: RAND tabulations from 5 percent MEDS-EDD microdata match file.

Figure 4.5—Percentage of Entering Cohorts Working by Calendar Year and Time Since Entering Welfare

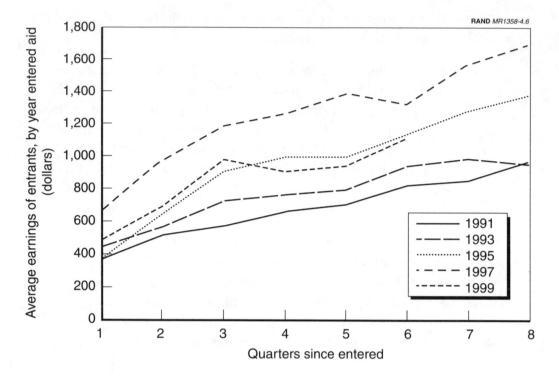

SOURCE: RAND tabulations from 5 percent MEDS-EDD microdata match file.

Figure 4.6—Average Earnings of Entrants to Welfare by Calendar Year and Time Since Entering Welfare

leavers than for current recipients (presumably because average earnings of new entrants who are still recipients are higher than average earnings for recent leavers).

Thus, the analytic approach of exploring cohorts of entrants in addition to cohorts of leavers appears promising. We will use it in our comparisons of the effects of county WTW programs in next year's report. Those estimates will benefit from data describing more post-CalWORKs quarters with more complete reporting of earnings.

Medi-Cal Take-Up Among Leavers

While federal welfare reform was intended to move current welfare recipients into the workforce and off welfare, Medicaid (Medi-Cal in California) coverage was intended to continue (Haskins, 1999). Continuing and extending pre-PRWORA policies, federal and California welfare reform broadened eligibility of welfare leavers for Medi-Cal.

Figure 4.7 tabulates the success of CWDs in providing Medi-Cal to leavers. To emphasize the observed changes, each line refers to a number of months since leaving welfare and the x-axis measures calendar time (unlike Figures 4.2 and 4.3).[11]

Immediately on leaving welfare (i.e., at one month, the top line), a high proportion of leavers have Medi-Cal coverage: 74 percent in 1994 and around 90 percent today. This is a deliberate policy resulting from the 1982 Edwards v. Kizer decision, which directed CWDs to place welfare leavers in the "Edwards Hold" (EH) until their continued eligibility for Medi-Cal is redetermined. Consistent with that decision, coverage immediately after leaving welfare increased sharply in the early 1990s and stays high.

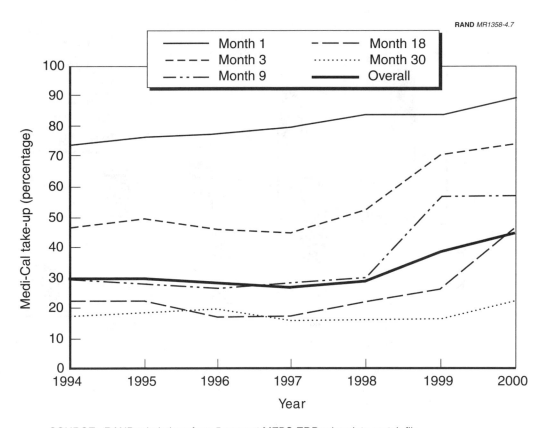

SOURCE: RAND tabulations from 5 percent MEDS-EDD microdata match file.

Figure 4.7—Medi-Cal Coverage of Welfare Leavers by Months Since Leaving Welfare and Calendar Year

---

[11]To minimize the effects of seasonality, we plotted the average rate for each year (defined as July–June) and a linear trend between these annual averages.

Coverage levels then drop with time since leaving welfare.[12] Today, only about 74 percent of welfare recipients have Medi-Cal coverage three months after leaving; 57 percent have coverage at nine months; 46 percent have coverage at 18 months; and 22 percent have coverage at 30 months. At all durations past one month, there has been a sharp and continuing increase with CalWORKs (i.e., beginning in 1998).

Figure 4.8 disaggregates the coverage by specific Medi-Cal program. It shows coverage at one, three, nine, 18, and 30 months after leaving welfare by program on the eve of CalWORKs (July 1996 to June 1997) and the most recent period for which data are available (July 1999 to June 2000). Consistent with Figure 4.7,

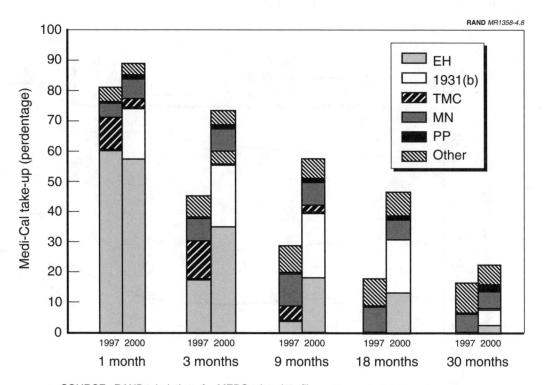

SOURCE: RAND tabulations for MEDS microdata file.

NOTE: EH = Edwards Hold; TMC = Transitional Medi-Cal; MN = Medically Needy programs; PP = Percentage Programs.

Figure 4.8—Medi-Cal Coverage of Welfare Leavers by Months Since Leaving Welfare and Calendar Year, Disaggregated by Program

---

[12]Everyone on welfare is automatically covered by Medi-Cal. Therefore, unlike Figures 4.1 through 4.6, which include those who return to cash assistance, Figures 4.7 and 4.8 exclude individuals who have returned to welfare.

Figure 4.8 shows that Medi-Cal coverage rises between the two years at each interval since leaving welfare.

When we consider the specific Medi-Cal programs, we find a more subtle story. In the period immediately after the passage of CalWORKs, while the California Department of Health Services (CDHS) revised the regulations governing Medi-Cal coverage for welfare leavers, CWDs were instructed to place all welfare leavers into the EH category, guaranteeing continued coverage until new guidelines could be determined. Most counties followed this direction, but some continued to process new welfare leavers under the existing guidelines. Once CDHS issued preliminary guidance about how to process Medi-Cal for welfare leavers, some counties began to unwind their EH cases. Some did so after receiving further guidance, and some still had large numbers of cases in EH into SFY 1999-2000. Thus, while the EH category is supposed to be used only for a month or two, in 2000, 35 percent of those at three months, 18 percent of those at nine months, 13 percent of those at 18 months, and about 3 percent of those at 30 months were still in EH. This sharp increase in EH coverage and delayed processing of the backlog of cases in that status explains some of the post-CalWORKs increase in Medi-Cal enrollment among welfare leavers.

Other factors are also at work. To provide expanded coverage for welfare leavers, PRWORA extended eligibility for Medicaid (Medi-Cal in California) coverage to anyone with income low enough to make them eligible for cash assistance under the pre-reform rules. This new eligibility criterion, known as 1931(b) (which also includes current welfare recipients), was intended to eliminate loss of Medicaid/Medi-Cal as a reason for not leaving welfare.

In California, 1931(b) coverage for welfare leavers began to be implemented in many counties in April 1999, as cases in EH were being processed. As intended, many people with EH coverage were shifted to 1931(b) coverage. Because the 1931(b) category is not time-limited, leavers who would have received only temporary coverage after leaving cash aid before CalWORKs can continue their Medi-Cal coverage under 1931(b) as long as they remain income-eligible.

In addition, federal legislation has mandated Transitional Medi-Cal (TMC) since 1988. TMC provides Medi-Cal for 12 months for welfare leavers. As allowed by federal statute and with state funds, California provides TMC benefits for an additional 12 months for adults. However, despite this extended eligibility, and unlike enrollment in other programs, enrollment in TMC has declined since CalWORKs implementation. The increase in take-up rates overall is thus not the result of longer or higher participation in TMC. There is reason to believe, though, that the decline in TMC may be the temporary result of the timing of processing the EH cases and the roll-out of the 1931(b) program. That is, leavers are eligible for TMC after receiving 1931(b) coverage as well as after leaving CalWORKs. (Prior to CalWORKs, TMC was available only as people left welfare.) Thus, a leaver may leave welfare, continue Medi-Cal coverage through 1931(b), and increase her earnings enough to make her ineligible for 1931(b), but she may still be eligible for TMC. The 1931(b) category thus can augment TMC. In fact, although enrollment levels are still low, TMC rates have risen since 1999 in the later months after leaving welfare.

Some of the rise in Medi-Cal take-up rates is the result of an increase in coverage through the Medically Needy (MN) program. Eligibility for MN is based on the criteria for the AFDC or SSI programs. Like 1931(b), MN is not a time-limited program. In fact, the increase in MN coverage appears to have supplemented the participation in the 1931(b) program. MN enrollment rose most in the period between the beginning of CalWORKs and the enactment of the 1931(b) program, the same period in which CDHS was clarifying 1931(b) regulations and Medi-Cal take-up procedures under CalWORKs. This is particularly true for counties that did not retain people in the EH category. In addition, coverage under the MN program leveled off after the implementation of 1931(b).

In summary, Medi-Cal coverage levels among welfare leavers have increased sharply since CalWORKs was enacted, but coverage is far from universal (about 57 percent at nine months and 22 percent after 30 months), and it declines relatively quickly with time since leaving aid. In interpreting these results, it is important to note that Medi-Cal is not the only source of health insurance coverage for this population. Some of the children are covered by a different government health insurance program, Healthy Families (California's Child Health Insurance Program (CHIP)). We are currently negotiating with the Managed Risk Medical Insurance Board, which administers Healthy Families, to gain access to their individual-level records for analysis. Such access would allow us to add Healthy Families as a category of coverage in our calculations.

In addition, national studies suggest that more than one-fourth of welfare leavers and one-third of those working are covered by private health insurance (Garrett and Holahan, 2000). Thus, overall health insurance coverage rates are higher than the Medi-Cal coverage rates reported here. The evaluation's household survey will provide direct evidence on coverage from Healthy Families, employers, and other non-Medi-Cal sources.

Outcomes for All Single-Parent Households

Proponents of federal welfare reform argued that one of its effects would be to discourage potential welfare recipients from ever entering the welfare system. Consistent with this expectation, we showed in Section 3 that about half of the welfare caseload decline results from lower rates of entry into welfare. Nevertheless, the tabulations in Section 2 and the earlier part of this section do not consider outcomes for this group. Part of the reason is lack of data—potential entrants never appear in the administrative data systems that are the focus of the analyses in this report.

In this section, we use the March Current Population Survey (CPS)[13]—a large national survey of the entire population—to explore outcomes for those at risk of going on welfare, whether they are currently on welfare, have recently left welfare, or are at risk of entering welfare. Following standard practice in the literature, we consider the "at risk" group to be single-mother households (i.e., an adult woman and one or more children, but no adult male).[14] This is the group most likely to be on welfare.

Specifically, we consider employment (Figure 4.9), earnings (Figure 4.10), and poverty status (Figure 4.11) of all single-mother households for California and for the rest of the nation. It is important to note that the total sample for California comprises about 5,000 households. In most years, about 500 single-mother households are surveyed in California, and about 5,000 in the nation as a whole. Thus, the California estimates are subject to considerable sampling variability, and small year-to-year differences often do not represent real differences in outcomes.

Figures 4.9, 4.10, and 4.11 all tell a consistent story. In California and in the rest of the nation, single-mother households are more likely to work, have rising earnings, and have falling poverty rates. These patterns continue and accelerate longer-term trends. Furthermore, the patterns for California are broadly similar to those for the rest of the nation, although (as with the caseload) there is some evidence that the improvements in California began later.

The falling poverty rates (Figure 4.11) are in contrast to the concerns of some opponents of federal welfare reform who claimed that reform would cause an explosion of poverty. The recent (1997 to 1999) year-to-year declines in poverty in single-mother households are among the largest ever recorded. If sampling

---

[13]See Appendix B for a description of the CPS.

[14]The sample includes anyone who is single, female, and the head of a family or subfamily, where family is defined as a household having at least one dependent child.

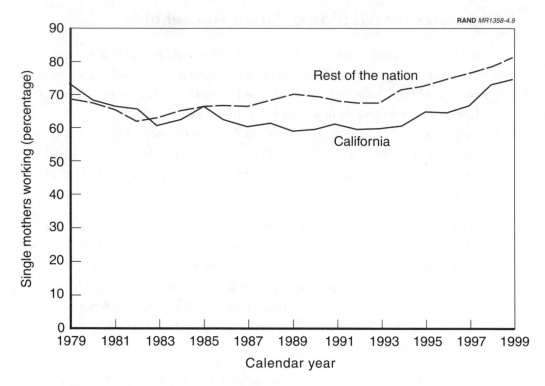

SOURCE: RAND tabulations from March CPS files.

Figure 4.9—Employment of Single-Mother Households, California and the Nation as a Whole by Year

variability is taken into account, the levels and patterns are identical to those in the nation as a whole.

Possible Explanations for the Descriptive Findings

What explains these trends for leavers? We next discuss some of the possible causes for the decreases in return to cash assistance, increases in employment and earnings, and decreases in poverty rates; we then turn to causes for the increase in Medi-Cal take-up rates.

Decreases in Return to Cash Aid, Increases in Employment and Earnings, and Decreases in Poverty Rates

We have already reviewed some probable causal factors in earlier sections. For example, many of the factors that might cause a decline in the caseload—in particular, tougher work requirements, time limits, the federal EITC, and the

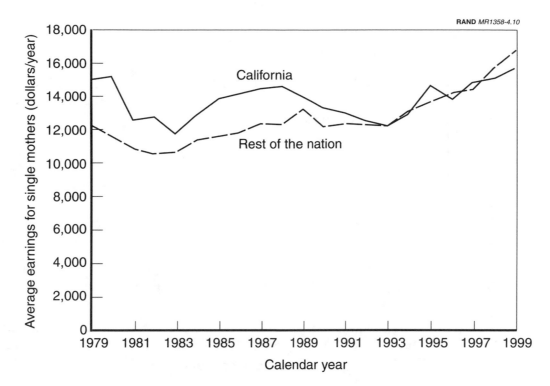

SOURCE: RAND tabulations from March CPS files.

Figure 4.10—Average Earnings of Single-Mother Households, California and the Nation as a Whole by Year

improving economy—would also be expected to cause a decline in return to cash assistance.

Similarly, many of the factors that might cause an increase in employment and earnings among current recipients—in particular, a work-first approach to WTW services, an improving economy, and the federal EITC—would also be expected to lead to improvements in employment and earnings for leavers.

In addition, the Work Pays reforms and their extensions in the CalWORKs reforms would be expected to have the indirect effect of raising earnings among welfare leavers. Since these reforms raise the earnings level at which a case becomes income-ineligible for cash assistance, leavers might be expected to have higher earnings on average when they finally leave welfare.[15]

_____

[15]Time limits, however, work in the opposite direction. To "bank" months of future eligibility for cash assistance, cases with relatively high earnings and thus low benefits might choose to leave welfare, even though they remain eligible for cash assistance. Some caseworkers report advising recipients to do this. Grogger (2000) finds some evidence for such anticipatory behavior.

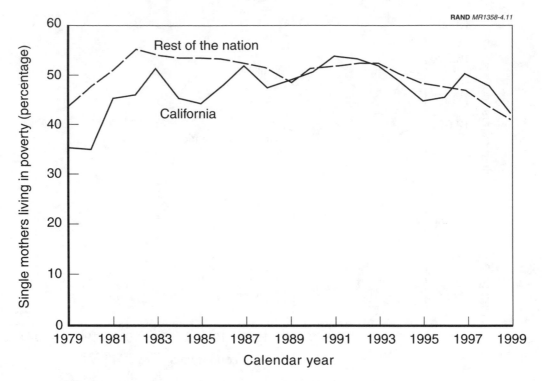

SOURCE: RAND tabulations from March CPS files.

Figure 4.11—Single-Mother Households in Poverty, California and the Nation as a Whole by Year

Some of the results presented here are consistent with a major role for welfare programs. While more analysis is needed, an effect on employment and earnings seems clearer in the tabulations for cohorts of entrants than in those for current recipients or leavers. Such an effect could be consistent with the experimental findings from MDRC's evaluation of work-first programs.

Many of the improvements in employment and earnings appear to date back to about 1994. Employment, average earnings, and the proportion of earnings greater than the minimum wage actually fell with time off aid for the 1990 cohort. Conversely, these measures rose (perhaps more than in earlier cohorts) for the 1994 cohort.

The implication that much of the improvement was the result of the economy is consistent with the lack of major reforms to WTW programs prior to CalWORKs (except for the 1995 GAIN reforms). The benefit cuts of the early 1990s may also have stimulated recipients to find work. Still, the preliminary evidence suggests a significant increase in employment and earnings with the implementation of CalWORKs. More data and more analysis over the coming year will enable us to make better estimates of relative effects.

Finally, since the poverty measure used here is dominated by labor earnings, the decreases in poverty are probably caused by the same factors that explain the increases in employment and earnings—the economy, the increase in the EITC, and, in the most recent period, welfare reform. National analyses suggest that these increases for single-mother households are much larger than the corresponding increases for single women without children or married women, and that they are also larger for less-educated women (e.g., Eissa and Liebman, 1995; Eissa and Hoynes, 1998; Ellwood, 1999). Since, unlike business cycle changes that affect everyone, the EITC and changes in welfare policy affect only families with children and low earnings, these differentials suggest the importance of the federal EITC and welfare reform, above and beyond the effect of the improving economy.[16]

Increases in Medi-Cal Take-up Rates

Only policy changes at the federal and state level and program changes at the county level seem to be plausible explanations of the sharp increase in Medi-Cal coverage under CalWORKs. As we saw above, Medi-Cal coverage in the post-CalWORKs periods has two phases. The early months after leaving welfare—as well as the first year to 18 months after CalWORKs was enacted—are dominated by slow county processing of EH cases, while the later months and the most recent year appear to reflect clarification of CDHS guidelines, positive changes in CWD policies and procedures, and the efforts of individual caseworkers. The only apparent explanation for the rise in take-up rates at these later stages is the multilevel effort to increase Medi-Cal take-up among leavers. This effort includes the new programs provided by federal and California legislation, CDSS's and CDHS's strong policies to encourage take-up, and strong efforts on the part of CWDs to enroll leavers initially and to keep them enrolled through time.

How these efforts will affect take-up rates in the near future is less clear. The processing of the remaining EH backlog and prompt processing of new EH cases (within one to two months, as was done in the pre-PRWORA period) will decrease Medi-Cal coverage rates, especially in months three to six after welfare exit. However, expanding outreach efforts and streamlined processes for maintaining Medi-Cal eligibility (in particular, increasing the time between mandatory recertifications) should raise Medi-Cal take-up immediately after EH coverage ceases and should also increase the probability of remaining on Medi-Cal as time since welfare exit increases.

---

[16]On the EITC, see Hotz and Scholz, 2000; see also Meyer and Rosenbaum (1999, 2000) and Ellwood (1999).

5. Conclusions and Next Steps

As noted in Section 1, this is the first of two reports on the impact of CalWORKs. It describes outcomes under CalWORKs through the summer of 2000 and begins the process of explaining the observed variation in outcomes—through time, between California and other states, and among California's counties. This concluding section summarizes the findings to date and discusses directions for additional analyses for the second and final impact analysis.

Conclusions

The impact analysis addresses three questions: (1) What has happened to the outcomes of interest? (2) Why do outcomes vary across time, between California and the other states, and among California's counties? and (3) Were the program changes made worth the cost? This report addresses the first and part of the second question (but does not consider intercounty variations). Here, we review our findings.

What Has Happened to Outcomes of Interest?

In the conceptual model of Section 1 (Figure 1.1), we argued that CalWORKs legislation could indirectly affect the outcomes of interest through the county welfare programs themselves and, in particular, through the process of implementing the CalWORKs model. We find (as shown in Section 2) that rates of participation in WTW activities—and, in particular, work—are rising. Absolute levels of participation, however, are low. Less than a third of all adults in single-parent cases are participating even at the federally required number of hours per week (25 hours, 20 for those with a child under six years of age). The corresponding fraction at the required state number of hours per week (32 hours) is less than a quarter. Among those not working, the corresponding fraction is much lower. It appears that as of the period described by the available data, county programs had had only limited success in involving those not yet ready for unsubsidized employment. Developing more-effective programs is an ongoing area of CWD activity.

When we look at how the caseload and outcomes for welfare leavers have changed over the past decade, we see (as shown in Sections 3 and 4) that the observed trends are nearly uniformly positive. Since its peak in mid-1995, the caseload has declined at about 1 percent per month, so that today it is about half its peak level. The decline in the caseload results equally from decreases in the rate of entrance into welfare and increases in the rate of exit from welfare. Finally, we note that while California's 43 percent decline in caseload is large, it is smaller than that of the nation as a whole (60 percent), and some states report declines of 80 percent or more.

Findings for the other outcomes also reflect nearly continuous and substantial improvement since the early 1990s, although in some cases the absolute levels remain low. Employment and earnings are up among both welfare recipients and welfare leavers, rates of return to welfare among welfare leavers are falling, Medi-Cal take-up among welfare leavers is rising, and poverty in single-mother families and for all children is falling.

What Caused These Outcomes?

Our descriptive analyses clearly show that most of the trends are positive. The next question is, What causes the positive trends we are seeing? It seems unlikely that county WTW programs are the major cause of the long-term (i.e., from the mid-1990s) decline in caseload and increases in employment and earnings. The timing is wrong. The improvements in almost all the outcomes date back to the early 1990s, well before the passage of CalWORKs and the consequent increase in spending by the counties and delivery of a significantly higher level of WTW services to recipients. Furthermore, while we would expect county WTW programs to affect primarily exits from welfare, about half of the caseload decrease results from the decline of entrants into welfare.

There is some evidence of accelerating improvements for some outcomes (exit rates from welfare, employment from entry into welfare) in the most recent periods. These recent improvements may result from the new CalWORKs programs. Understanding this recent experience and how it unfolds past the data available for this report will be a major focus of our second impact analysis report a year from now.

What else might explain the outcomes? Like the national literature on the effects of welfare reform, our answers to these questions are preliminary and in some cases speculative. It seems clear that a major role should be assigned to the economy. With a better economy, those off welfare have better job prospects, thus lowering the entrance rate onto welfare; those on welfare are more likely to find jobs, thus raising the participation rate and the exit rate from welfare; and those who have left welfare are more likely to be employed and less likely to return to welfare, thus lowering reentrance rates to welfare. Finally, because recipients have higher incomes, fewer children and families will be in poverty. Based on our analyses, the improved economy appears to explain about half of the state's caseload decline from its peak in March 1995, much of the variation in caseload decline across the counties, and some of the differential decline between California and the rest of the nation. As part of the evaluation, we are now performing equivalent analyses of the effect of the economy on other outcomes (e.g., employment and earnings of current recipients and leavers, by time since entering welfare).

Some role should also be assigned to nonwelfare policies. The national literature suggests that the massive expansions of the federal EITC in the late 1980s and early 1990s, combined with increases in California's minimum wage and the Work Pays reforms to the benefit structure (augmented further by the CalWORKs legislation), have probably all contributed to higher levels of employment and earnings for current recipients and welfare leavers. In addition, by making work more attractive, these changes have probably also helped to shrink the caseload. Moreover, the increase in the take-up rate of Medi-Cal among welfare leavers is plausibly related to the adoption of new Medi-Cal programs and intensive information and casework efforts on the part of CDSS and CWDs.

Finally, some of the more recent declines probably result from changes to state policies under CalWORKs. We have already noted the likelihood that the Work Pays reforms and their extensions as part of CalWORKs have increased work among current recipients. In addition, the new environment, with its new message that program participation is expected of (nearly) every adult, has probably contributed to the caseload decline, discouraging entrance and encouraging faster exit.

That said, the national econometric evidence and simulations for California suggest that while the details of the CalWORKs legislation—participation-rate requirements, sanction policy, time-limit policy, and benefit structure—explain some of the caseload decline, they probably also partly explain why California's caseload has declined less than that in other states. Compared with the TANF reforms in other states and the immediate pre-TANF waiver reforms, the CalWORKs legislation made less dramatic changes in welfare in California. In many other states, the new TANF programs or immediate pre-TANF waivers brought earlier and more strictly enforced participation-rate requirements (especially among those not working): full-family sanctions—more swiftly and surely applied than in California, and shorter lifetime time limits—with earlier start dates; and cessation of payments for both adult(s) and children when the time limit is reached. Just as it seems likely that the CalWORKs policy changes explain some of the changes in outcomes, especially the caseload decline, it seems likely that the more dramatic policy changes in other states would have caused larger changes in outcomes, in particular, a larger decline in caseloads.

However, whether the state's smaller caseload decline that has apparently resulted from these policy choices is a cause for concern is far from clear. Lower benefit levels and stricter sanctions and time limits would imply fewer monetary resources for the state's poorest families. It seems likely that there is a tradeoff; programs that would decrease the caseload would probably also leave some children worse off.

The policy choices in the CalWORKs legislation are broadly consistent with California's policies in the pre-PRWORA period. Arguably, they reflect the state's balancing of the higher safety net for children against the resulting larger welfare caseload, including its higher cost and greater dependency. If the perception of the appropriate balance has shifted, then cutting the welfare benefit, more strictly imposing the universal-participation requirement, streamlining the conciliation process, increasing the maximum sanction, cutting the time limit, and removing the continuing payment to the child(ren) would each probably cut the welfare caseload, but at the cost of significantly decreasing the financial resources available to support children.

Were the Changes Worth the Cost?

We defer addressing the cost/benefit question until next year. In this report, we have laid a foundation for that analysis by describing program outcomes (so that we better understand program benefits). As mentioned above, the implementation of WTW programs occurred too late to be a major factor in the earlier changes observed in our data. An additional year of experience will be particularly important in understanding the effects of county WTW programs. As of the summer of 2000, those programs were settling into steady state. Once we have another year of results with the programs in steady-state operation and more post-welfare experience for leavers, we will be able to build on our foundation with additional analyses of costs and benefits.

Next Steps

This report has concentrated on describing trends in California, compared with other states and between California's counties through approximately the summer of 2000—later for some measures, earlier for others. It has also begun the process of trying to understand the effects of CalWORKs and other factors on the observed variation—through time, between states, and among California's counties.

This leaves four tasks for the coming year and our second and final report on the impact of CalWORKs. First, as mentioned above, the second report will incorporate another year of experience with the CalWORKs programs and with the PRWORA programs in other states. In particular, the present report analyzes data for relatively little time off aid for those who left with the implementation of the CalWORKs reforms, both the policies and the programs. These additional data are particularly important in view of the evidence of accelerating improvements in outcomes toward the end of the data analyzed for this report, presumably as the reformed and expanded county CalWORKs programs were having their effects.

Moreover, with another year of data, we will see the effects of cases in more states reaching time limits. Finally, especially with respect to the employment and earnings information from the MEDS/EDD match, we will explore the completeness of the data by cross-checking reported earnings against other sources (e.g., our household survey) that include different types of income—out-of-state, income from independent contracting, and earnings of other family members.

Second, this report has explored a relatively narrow set of outcomes—work activities participation rates, caseloads, employment and earnings of leavers, poverty. In the remainder of the project, we will consider a wider range of outcomes. In particular, separate reports will present results from the first and then the second wave of our survey of current and recent welfare recipients. That survey is collecting information on experiences in interacting with CWDs and broader measures of household well-being.

Third, this report begins the task of understanding the causes of the trends in outcomes for California and differential outcomes for California versus the rest of the nation. Over the next year, we will extend and expand these analyses, also drawing on the rapidly expanding national literature on these issues.

Fourth, the second report will examine the differential effects of the welfare programs in each of California's 58 counties. As we noted earlier, those programs are only now settling down into a post-surge steady state, and quality improvements are continuously being considered and implemented.

Appendix

A. Overview of Factors That Might Affect Outcomes

This appendix provides additional details on the possible determinants of outcomes under CalWORKs. Unless otherwise noted, the information is drawn from the U.S. Committee on Ways and Means *Green Book* for 1996 and 2000.

Federal Reforms

The recent history of welfare reform begins with the 1988 Family Support Act (FSA), which was based on the concept of mutual responsibility and established the Job Opportunities and Basic Skills (JOBS) program (in California, the GAIN program (discussed further below)) to provide education and training for welfare recipients and assistance in finding employment. Also, beginning in the late 1980s and accelerating during the early 1990s, the federal government granted to states a wide-ranging set of waivers to modify their welfare programs, including (1) changes to the benefit structure to encourage work; (2) stronger sanctions for nonparticipation in mandatory WTW activities; and (3) lifetime time limits on receipt of cash assistance.

These early reform steps culminated in 1996 in the sweeping welfare reform of PRWORA. That legislation replaced the AFDC program with the TANF program. PRWORA limited lifetime federally funded assistance in a TANF program to five years, and it devolved nearly complete discretion to the states in designing their TANF programs. To implement this new discretion, most federal funding for state welfare programs was rolled into a single flexible TANF block grant. Table A.1 summarizes the caseload decline, work participation rates, and the benefit structure—the cash benefit for a family of three and maximum earnings at which a long-term recipient is still eligible for cash assistance.

CALWORKS Reforms

CalWORKs is California's TANF plan. The Act (AB 1542) was enacted August 11, 1997, to implement PRWORA, enacted August 22, 1996.

Table A.1

Caseload Decline, Work Participation Rates, and Benefit Structure

State	Persons (1/95)	Persons (12/99)	% Change	TANF Work Participation Rate, FY 1999 (overall)	Cash Benefit[a] ($)	Maximum Earnings[b] ($)
AL	121,837	58,352	-52.1	37.4	164	205
AK	37,264	23,303	-37.5	46.0	923	1,641
AZ	195,082	87,909	-54.9	32.1	347	586
AR	65,325	30,912	-52.7	23.7	204	697
CA	2,692,202	1,333,820	-50.5	42.2	626	1,477
CO	110,742	30,263	-72.7	36.4	356	511
CT	170,719	69,214	-59.5	47.4	543	1,157
DE	26,314	18,471	-29.8	24.9	338	958
DC	72,330	48,442	-33.0	26.7	379	858
FL	657,313	171,874	-73.9	31.6	303	806
GA	388,913	137,241	-64.7	17.6	280	514
HI	65,207	42,239	-35.2	41.1	570	1,363
ID	24,050	2,523	-89.5	43.7	293	625
IL	710,032	288,609	-59.4	60.4	377	1,131
IN	197,225	98,410	-50.1	33.3	288	378
IA	103,108	51,892	-49.7	54.8	426	1,065
KS	81,504	37,241	-54.3	57.3	403	762
KY	193,722	90,806	-53.1	38.1	262	646
LA	258,180	95,176	-63.1	29.4	190	310
ME	60,973	30,838	-49.4	54.9	461	1,103
MD	227,887	75,549	-66.8	11.2	417	642
MA	286,175	107,542	-62.4	27.8	565	1,045
MI	612,224	218,055	-64.4	43.8	459	774
MN	180,490	114,311	-36.7	36.9	789	1,400
MS	146,319	34,412	-76.5	27.0	170	458
MO	259,595	126,723	-51.2	28.2	292	382
MT	34,313	14,479	-57.8	92.3	468	824
NE	42,038	28,294	-32.7	34.7	364	669
NV	41,846	15,117	-63.9	34.8	348	438
NH	28,671	14,287	-50.2	29.9	600	1,200
NJ	321,151	139,308	-56.6	30.3	424	848
NM	105,114	79,071	-24.8	27.6	439	1,028
NY	1,266,350	760,931	-39.9	36.3	577	1,157
NC	317,836	106,836	-66.4	16.0	272	750
ND	14,920	7,589	-49.1	31.7	457	1,014
OH	629,719	254,550	-59.6	53.7	373	996
OK	127,336	38,995	-69.4	42.9	292	704
OR	107,610	58,600	-45.5	96.7	460	616
PA	611,215	267,891	-56.2	16.2	403	806
RI	62,407	47,225	-24.3	28.8	554	1,278
SC	133,567	39,188	-70.7	44.7	201	678
SD	17,652	7,005	-60.3	46.5	430	628
TN	281,982	163,839	-41.9	41.1	185	949
TX	765,460	342,810	-55.2	27.3	197	317
UT	47,472	26,074	-45.1	44.0	451	1,002
VT	27,716	16,695	-39.8	(c)	622	979
VA	189,493	78,182	-58.7	41.1	291	1,157
WA	290,940	158,062	-45.7	40.3	546	1,092
WV	107,668	28,850	-73.2	25.6	328	547
WI	214,404	44,600	-79.2	80.1	673	673
WY	15,434	1,288	-91.7	57.7	340	540
U.S. total	13,930,953	6,274,555	-55.0			

[a]For a family of three with no earnings in 2000.

[b]Earnings above which a recipient is ineligible for cash assistance in the thirteenth month, January 2000.

[c]Not subject to participation-rate requirements.

California was among the last states to reform its welfare program in response to PRWORA. The federal reporting requirements and work participation standards went into effect October 1, 1997, less than two months after the enactment of the legislation. But some provisions of CalWORKs (including time limits) did not become effective until January 1998. Still other provisions did not become effective until the state had certified the county's CalWORKs plans; for most counties, this occurred in March 1998. Counties were not required to "enroll" recipients into CalWORKs until the end of December 1998. In many counties, activities beyond enrollment (appraisal, Job Club, assessment, post-assessment, WTW activities) did not begin in volume until late 1998 or early 1999 (see Klerman et al., 2001).

Time Limits

While other states adopted shorter time limits, California enacted the longest time limit allowed under the federal PRWORA legislation, a 60-month lifetime limit on cash aid receipt. In California, federal time-limit clocks began to tick in December 1997 (the month following the approval of California's pro-forma TANF plan, allowing the state to draw down federal TANF dollars). However, the CalWORKs legislation, which was passed in August 1997, specified that state time-limit clocks did not begin to tick until January 1998. In addition, unlike most other states (but like most other large states), after the time limit, California excludes only the adults from an assistance unit. Payments for the child(ren) (to an adult) continue.

Participation Requirements

PRWORA requires that within 24 months of aid receipt, an individual must be working or in community service. Furthermore, the minimum number of hours required to satisfy this requirement rises through time.

The requirements in CalWORKs appear to be stronger than those in the federal statute. CalWORKs has an individual participation requirement immediately on receipt of cash assistance, and new recipients (since January 1998) must be either employed or in community service within 18 months of receipt of assistance.

However, this requirement is, in practice, usually weaker than that of the federal requirement, for three reasons. First, the clock does not begin to tick until after the signing of a WTW plan. Such a plan is signed only by recipients who do not find a job (with sufficient hours) before or during Job Club. Those who find a job or are sanctioned do not sign a plan, so their 18-month clock never starts to tick.

In practice, a plan is often not signed until well after six months, so the 18-month clock usually lasts well beyond 24 months after initial receipt of welfare. Intervals until signing a plan were particularly long while agencies were ramping up to serve the pre-CalWORKs cases (see Klerman et al., 2000). Second, counties have the option of certifying that no job is currently available and extending the 18-month clock to 24 months (again, from the signing of the WTW plan). Finally, recipients as of the start of CalWORKs (in most counties, March 1998) were all granted 24 months.

Expanded Services

CalWORKs provides for and funds an extended suite of services. Job Club was extended to be nearly universal. Substance-abuse, mental-health, and domestic-violence services were made available. Funding levels were high enough not to be a constraint. Department of Labor Welfare-to-Work (DoL WtW) funding and dedicated funding for California's Community College system implied that there were generous funds for education and training.

As Klerman et al. (2001) discuss, the roll-out of the new county WTW programs took time. California started drawing federal TANF dollars during SFY 1996–1997, the CalWORKs legislation passed in August 1997, and some of the new policies went into effect in January 1998. The new county WTW programs, however, started to affect recipients only later.

County WTW plans were submitted and approved in the early months of calendar year 1998, and enrollment of recipients in the new programs began about March 1998. Enrollment lasted through about the end of calendar year 1998.

Total county WTW expenditures provide a useful proxy for the roll-out of county WTW programs. Figure A.1 shows that quarterly county WTW expenditures were relatively flat (at slightly more than $50 million) until the last quarter of SFY 1997–1998 (i.e., April to June 1998), when they increased by 50 percent (to $78 million). Expenditures have grown sharply, but inconsistently, since then. In the most recent period for which data are available (SFY 1999–2000 Q4), quarterly expenditures were $196 million, nearly four times their level of three years earlier.

These expenditure data suggest that county WTW programs have rolled out progressively over SFY 1997–1998 Q4 to the present. Our fieldwork (Zellman et al., 1999a,b; Klerman et al., 2001) suggests that there was little increase in the intensity of WTW services until late in calendar year 1998 (SFY 1998–1999 Q2) at

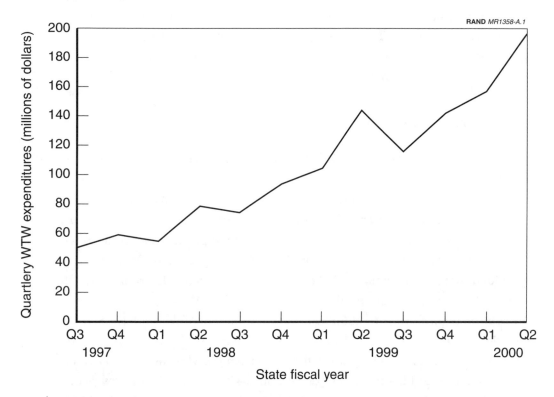

SOURCE: RAND tabulations from county expense claim file.

Figure A.1—Quarterly County WTW Expenditures

the earliest. Most of the observed increase in expenditure went to hiring and training new staff, with more actual services to recipients following one to two quarters later.

Earlier Welfare Reforms

GAIN

Originally established in 1986, GAIN was California's pre-TANF WTW program. With the passage of the federal 1988 FSA, GAIN became California's JOBS program. Initially, the program had a strong education-and-training focus. A random-assignment evaluation by MDRC (Riccio et al., 1994) suggested that an alternative program design in Riverside County that was focused on "work first" had larger impacts on employment, earnings, welfare payments, and the welfare caseload than did the more education-and-training-focused programs in the other evaluated counties. Consistent with those findings, AB 1371 (Weggeland, approved August 3, 1995) refocused the program away from its earlier emphasis on human-capital development (HCD) (i.e., education and training) toward a labor-force attachment (LFA) strategy focused on Job Club; however, implementation of these reforms appears to have been only partial at the time CalWORKs was implemented in early 1998.

Fill-the-Gap Budgeting

Chapter 97, Statutes of 1991 (SB 724, Maddy), made several changes to California's AFDC program. These changes included the California statutory approval for the changes that would be implemented as the Work Pays Demonstration Project after federal approval of California's 1115 waiver request (elimination of the 100 hour rule and extension of the $30 and one-third earned income disregard; see below). Of more immediate impact, that legislation provided that as of January 1992, the AFDC grant was to be determined by fill-the gap budgeting. Under fill-the-gap budgeting, the AFDC grant is determined by subtracting a recipient's countable income from the Minimum Basic Standard of Adequate Care (MBSAC; Welfare and Institution Code Section 10452 et seq., also known as the need standard) rather than from the Maximum Aid Payment (MAP; Welfare and Institutions Code Section 10450 et seq.). For low levels of countable income, the work incentive was somewhat stronger under the AFDC disregards in 1996–1997 than the $225 and one-half disregard created under CalWORKs (see below).

Work Pays

Under waivers from the federal government, California implemented the Work Pays Demonstration Project. The demonstration had several components, including cutting the cash benefit and waiving the 100-hour rule. Here, we discuss the changes in the benefit structure that were later continued and extended under CalWORKs.

Under the applicable federal statute (OBRA 1981), working welfare recipients kept the first $30 and then one-third of any additional earnings. However, the $30 provision lasted only one year, and the one-third provision lasted only four months (U.S. Department of Health and Human Services, 1996). Work Pays changed the regulations so that effective September 1, 1993, the "thirty and a third" provisions would remain in place indefinitely.

The expectation was that Work Pays would raise work effort. However, a randomized-trial evaluation failed to find any statistically significant effect on work activity or earnings for AFDC-FG cases and only limited evidence of an effect on time on aid (Becerra et al., 1996). Results for AFDC-U cases are slightly more supportive of the expectation of increased work effort (in one of the three counties). However, these results are inconsistent with other randomized-assignment work that finds strong employment and earnings effects of Work Pays-type reforms (e.g., Berlin et al., 2000).

Benefit Levels

By statute (Welfare and Institutions Code, Section 11453), California's aid payment includes a COLA based on the California Needs Index (CNI) computed by the Department of Finance. Special legislation in the 1990s suspended or modified the COLA in several years. In addition, in some years, cuts were made in the nominal benefit amount. The net effect of the benefit cuts and the COLA suspensions was that the real welfare benefit was cut by about 40 percent. Table A.2 gives a history of aid payments.

Other Policy Changes

EITC

First enacted in 1975, the federal EITC provides a refundable tax credit for those with low earnings. Today, federal expenditures on the EITC are larger than federal expenditures on TANF. The credit was indexed for inflation in 1987 and substantially expanded in 1990 and 1993 (as shown in Table A.3), such that the maximum credit of $983 in 1990 increased to $2,528 in 1994 and $3,816 in 1999. For a family with two children in 2000, the credit was 40 percent of earnings up to $9,700, resulting in a maximum credit of $3,888. The credit remains at that level through earnings of $12,700. Thereafter, it phases out at a rate of 21.06 percent, so that the credit is zero at earnings of $31,182.

The significant increase in the EITC is simultaneous with and complementary to (but for the most part statutorily distinct from) national welfare reform and the Work Pays reforms in California.

Since 1998, total credit amounts have been about $30 billion, several times the size of the TANF program. For a more complete discussion of the EITC, see U.S. Committee on Ways and Means, *Green Book*, 2000, p. 808ff, and Hotz and Scholz (2000).

Table A.2

History of the Statutory Aid Payment

SFY	Change in Index (percent)	COLA Change (percent)	Other Change to MAP (percent)	Nominal Total Change (percent)	Real Total Change (percent)	Other Info.
71–72		Introduced into law	Introduced into law	N/A	N/A	
72–73		None	1.10	1.10		(a)
73–74	2.83	2.83	None	2.83	0.00	
74–75	7.42	7.42	None	7.42	0.00	
75–76	12.18	12.18	None	12.18	0.00	
76–77	8.54	8.54	6.00	14.54	0.00	
77–78	5.24	5.24	None	5.24	0.00	
78–79	7.71	Suspended	None	None	-7.71	
79–80	6.91	15.16	None	15.16	8.25	(b)
80–81	—	15.48	-2.48	13.00	-2.48	(c)
81–82	11.10	9.20	None	9.20	-1.90	
82–83	6.20	Suspended	None	None	-6.20	
83–84	5.70	4.00	None	4.00	-1.70	
84–85	5.60	5.60	None	5.60	0.00	
85–86	5.70	5.70	None	5.70	0.00	
86–87	5.10	5.10	None	5.10	0.00	
87–88	2.60	2.60	None	2.60	0.00	
88–89	4.70	4.70	None	4.70	0.00	
89–90	4.61	4.61	None	4.61	0.00	
90–91	—	Suspended	None	None		(d)
91–92	5.49	Suspended	-4.40	-4.40	-9.89	
92–93	1.81	Suspended	-5.80	-5.80	-7.61	
93–94	2.37	Suspended	-2.70	-2.70	-5.07	
94–95	1.69	Suspended	None	None	-1.69	
95–96	1.48	Suspended	None	None	-1.48	
96–97	0.52		Region 1: -4.9; Region 2: -9.56		-5.42	(e)
97–98	2.60	Suspended	None	None	-2.60	(f)
98–99	2.84	2.84	None	2.84	0.00	
99–00	2.36	2.36	None	2.36	0.00	
00–01	2.96	2.96	None	2.96	0.00	

SOURCE: Michelle Carotti, CDSS, Estimates Office.

[a]Included to make up for an increase in sales tax.

[b]Includes catch-up from 1978–1979.

[c]New COLA measure.

[d]No index appears to have been computed; national CPI-U (Consumer Price Index–Urban Consumers) increased 4.68 percent in calendar year 1989.

[e]COLA changed to reflect 100 percent of CNI.

[f]CalWORKs implemented.

Table A.3

Federal EITC

Year	Maximum Credit Rate (percent)	Maximum Amount ($)
1977–78	10.0	400
1979–84	10.0	500
1985–86	14.0	550
1987	14.0	851
1988	14.0	874
1989	14.0	910
1990	14.7	983
1991	17.3	1,235
1992	18.4	1,384
1993	19.5	1,511
1994	30.0	2,528
1995	36.0	3,110
1996	40.0	3,556
1997	40.0	3,656
1998	40.0	3,756
1999	40.0	3,816
2000	40.0	3,888

NOTE: Values for families with two or more children.
SOURCE: U.S. Committee on Ways and Means, *Green Book*, 2000, p. 809.

Minimum Wage

Proposition 210 on the 1996 ballot raised California's minimum wage above the federal minimum wage. Nearly simultaneously, the 1996 Amendments to the federal Fair Labor Standards Act (FLSA) raised the federal minimum wage, but not to the level of California's (as shown in Table A.4). Then, in October 2000, a decision of the California Industrial Welfare Commission raised the minimum again, by one dollar an hour, in two steps, bringing California's minimum wage to the third highest in the country; only in Oregon and Washington are minimum wages higher ($6.50). For most purposes, the operative minimum wage is the maximum of the federal and state minimum wages.

For a more complete discussion of the minimum wage, see "Analysis of Proposition 210," at http://vote96.ss.ca.gov/Vote96/html/BP/210analysis.htm. For a discussion of the federal minimum wage, see "History of Changes to the FLSA," at http://www.dol.gov/dol/esa/public/minwage/coverage.htm; "Statement of the President on the Signing of the Small Business Job Protection Act of 1996," at http://www.dol.gov/dol/esa/public/minwage/signing.htm;

Table A.4

Minimum Wage

	Minimum Wage ($/hr)	
Date of Change	Federal	California
January 1, 1981	$3.35	—
April 1, 1990	$3.80	—
April 1, 1991	$4.25	—
October 1, 1996	$4.75	—
March 1, 1997	—	$5.00
September 1, 1997	$5.15	—
March 1, 1998	—	$5.75
January 1, 2001	—	$6.25
January 1, 2002	—	$6.75

and "Value of the Federal Minimum Wage, 1938-1997," at http://www.dol.gov/dol/esa/public/minwage/chart2.htm, which computes the real minimum wage.

Immigration Reform and Control Act (IRCA)

The 1986 Immigration Reform and Control Act (IRCA) appears to have had significant indirect effects on California's welfare caseload. IRCA granted an amnesty to undocumented aliens who could prove that they had been in the United States since 1982. As a result, more than 2.7 million immigrants were legalized, 1.6 million of them in California. Their regional distribution is far from uniform: 49 percent intended to live in Los Angeles County; 25 percent, in other Southern California Counties; 16 percent, in the Central Valley; 9 percent, in the Bay Area Counties; and only 1 percent, in the North and Mountain counties (see MaCurdy, Mancuso, and O'Brien-Strain, 2000, p. 30).

The original IRCA legislation specifically barred immigrants from receiving welfare for five years after legalization, most of which occurred in 1987 and 1988. MaCurdy, Mancuso, and O'Brien-Strain (2000) argue that IRCA would have stimulated additional immigration, since children born in the United States to such illegal immigrants would be eligible for cash assistance (although their parents would not), further increasing the child-only welfare population.

Medi-Cal

Medicaid is a joint state-federal program to provide health insurance to poor Americans. In California, the program is known as Medi-Cal. Prior to federal welfare reform, there were two primary routes onto Medi-Cal that are germane to our analysis: (1) everyone receiving cash assistance (i.e., AFDC) was categorically eligible for Medi-Cal and automatically enrolled, and (2) a series of

"Medicaid Expansions" made Medi-Cal available to many other poor children and some adults. Between 1986 and 1991, the Medi-Cal program was gradually expanded to cover pregnant women with children within some percentage of the poverty line. The extensions were largest for the youngest children in the poorest families.

With welfare reform, the details of the program changed, increasing eligibility for coverage. Under the 1931(b) provisions, anyone who would have been eligible for AFDC under the pre-reform rules remains eligible for Medi-Cal. In addition, PRWORA created the TMA program to extend Medi-Cal coverage for six months after the recipient leaves welfare. (In most cases, the coverage continues for a second six months.) This provision will end in September 2001.

Finally, the Balanced Budget Act of 1997 created the State Children's Health Insurance Program (S-CHIP), known in California as "Healthy Families." The S-CHIP program provides matching funds that the states can use in a variety of ways to extend health insurance to additional children in households with incomes below 200 percent of the federal poverty level (or, in some cases, up to 350 percent) who are not otherwise covered by Medicaid/Medi-Cal. In California, eligibility is limited to those with incomes below 250 percent of the poverty line. As of 1999, 187,854 children were enrolled in the standalone Healthy Families program, and another 34,497 children were enrolled through the Medi-Cal program.

The Economy

Statewide

California's economy went into a deep recession in the early 1990s. As shown earlier in Figure 3.4, the unemployment rate peaked in 1993 and has decreased sharply since then. California's recession was deeper than that of the nation as a whole, and the recovery occurred later.

Neither the recession nor the recovery was uniform across the state. The recession was deepest in Los Angeles and Southern California and barely noticed in the Bay Area. The recovery was likewise sharpest in Los Angeles and Southern California and barely noticed in Northern California.

B. Data Sources

In this appendix, we briefly describe the datasets used in this analysis. Additional detail on the datasets can be found in Haider et al. (2000). Table B.1 summarizes the datasets, and the following text provides additional detail on some issues.

Table B.1

Characteristics of Datasets

Name	Content	Period[a]	Frequency[b]
	County aggregate filings with CDSS		
CA 237	Caseload and aid payments	1/87–6/00	M
County Expense Claim (CEC)	Program expenses	1/92–6/00	Q
GAIN 25 - WTW 25	WTW activities	1/92–6/00	M
	Performance-bonus claims	1/98–6/00	Q
	Individual-level administrative data		
MEDS	Program participation	1/87–6/00	M
EDD	Covered earnings	1/92–6/00	Q
Q5	Quality-control data	7/97–6/99	M
	Survey data		
CPS	Household detail	4/76–4/99	A

[a]Period analyzed for this report. In some cases, more data exist that are not used here.
[b]M = monthly; Q = quarterly; A = annually.

County Aggregate Filings with CDSS

CWDs file regular reports with CDSS about their caseloads and aid payments (the CA 237 form) and their program expenditures (the County Expense Claim form). The first form is filed monthly, while the second one is filed quarterly. The analysis reported here uses data through October 2000 for the CA 237 and through June 2000 (second calendar quarter 2000/last quarter SFY 1999–2000) for the County Expense Claim.

The GAIN 25/WTW 25 data are the monthly county filings to the CDSS reporting the number of participants in each component of their WTW programs in the month covered. Here we use filings through June 2000. The GAIN 25/WTW 25 data are widely believed (by county officials, by state officials, and by the RAND team) to be of uneven quality. Data quality in the period from the start of CalWORKs through about April 2000 appears to be particularly bad. At about that date, the counties with EDS computer systems installed new software that appears to have improved reporting; however, the quality of the underlying data in those systems continues to be uneven (see Klerman et al. (1999) and the forthcoming third process analysis report).

In addition, this report uses some state filings to the federal DHHS-ACF. They include data on caseloads (through June 2000), work participation rates (through September 1999, i.e., FFY 1999), and expenditures (through FFY 1999).

Individual-Level Administrative Data

In addition to these aggregate filings, for some outcomes we analyze individual-level data, which allow for disaggregated analyses (e.g., by race, earnings level, or time since leaving welfare). In particular, for anyone ever on welfare, MEDS includes individual-level data on program participation (cash assistance and other Medi-Cal programs) for the period January 1987 through December 2000, and the MEDS-EDD match provides individual-level data on employment and earnings in covered employment for third quarter 1990 to third quarter 2000. For a small sample, the Q5 data contain detailed results from quality-control audits. Here we provide some additional detail on each of these three data sources.

MEDS. This source provides individual-level data on program participation (Medi-Cal, AFDC/CalWORKs, SSI, Food Stamps). The Food Stamps data are considered to be of uneven quality. The DHHS allows the MEDS or AFDC/CalWORKs data to be used for drawing the quality control sample, but the U.S. Department of Agriculture (USDA) does not allow the use of the Food Stamp data for that purpose.

One difficulty in using the MEDS data is that there is a processing lag in designating Medi-Cal claimants as AFDC/TANF recipients. This lag has two effects on our analysis: Results for the most recent months will be subject to updating as additional claims are entered into MEDS, and given the construction of our dataset, the lag causes a false periodicity in the data. However, because of the regularity in the processing lag, we are able to statistically rescale the data to account for it. See Haider et al. (2000) for further details.

The MEDS files are very large. Many of the analyses reported here are based on samples that are structured to maintain approximately equal numbers of observations in each county (or every observation in the smaller counties). Specifically, sampling (with a time-invariant sampling weight assigned to each person) is based on the county in which recipients are first observed receiving cash assistance.

EDD. The EDD provides employer individual-level filings to establish eligibility for UI, Disability Insurance (DI), and some components of the Personal Income Tax system. However, only covered employment and earnings are reported. This excludes earnings of federal government employees and the self-employed (including a large number of people in the murky "independent contractor" group) (see Hotz, Imbens, and Klerman, 2000). "Under-the-table income" is also not included. Finally, these data appear to accumulate quite slowly. We use the file available in mid-August 2000, which includes some data through June 2000. However, our comparisons of files across quarters suggest that in fact this file is only complete through September 1999.

Like the MEDS file, the matched MEDS-EDD file is very large. Therefore, many of the analyses here are based on the same samples used for the MEDS. In particular, the EDD data for 1990 to 1992 are available only for an approximately 17 percent subsample selected to make the number of observations in each county approximately equal. Other adults in sampled households are also included in the file to allow computation of household earnings (at least those of adults). This results in a file with earnings for approximately 20 percent of all individuals ever observed to receive welfare.

Q5. The Q5 system provides individual-level quality control audit data statewide for about 6,000 cases per year. These data are used to construct the official federal participation rates. As such, they include detailed information on program participation, earnings, and the aid payment. However, the Q5 files are too small (about 300 cases in the 19 largest counties) to allow county-level analyses. In this report, we provide tabulations from the final Q5 file for FFY 1999.

Survey Data

The aggregate filings and individual data files cover only a limited set of outcomes and include only current and recent welfare recipients. To analyze a broader set of outcomes or a broader population (i.e., all children of all single-parent households, regardless of recent receipt of welfare), we must use survey data. In this report, we analyze data from the Annual Demographic Supplement to the CPS. Conducted annually for several decades, the CPS collects detailed information about household income (and thus poverty status), family structure, and health insurance for about 50,000 households. The sample size in California is large enough to provide rough estimates for the state as a whole and some comparisons between the state and the rest of the nation. The sample is also large enough to reveal major trends (although considerable year-to-year variation resulting from sampling variability remains).

In addition, the evaluation is currently fielding a two-wave survey, the California Health and Social Services Survey (CHSSS). The CHSSS is a household survey of current and recent welfare recipients in the Statewide CalWORKs Evaluation's six focus counties that will provide information on outcomes not well measured in the available administrative data or in the CPS.[1] Results from the first wave will be released in a separate report; results from the second wave will be included in the second impact analysis report.

CPS. The CPS is a monthly national survey of about 50,000 households in the general American population. It includes both welfare recipients and non-welfare recipients; in California, it includes about 5,000 households or 10 percent of the U.S. population. Here, we analyze the March Demographic Supplement, which includes information on family structure, welfare receipt, and household income (for all sources). The reports in March of a year present outcomes for the previous calendar year.

---

[1]The six focus counties are Alameda, Butte, Fresno, Los Angeles, Sacramento, and San Diego.

C. Analytic Methods

This appendix presents a brief description of some of the analytic methods used to derive the results reported in the text. Further information on analytic methods can be found in the underlying technical reports cited in the opening footnotes of each section.

Q5-Based Approximation to the Federal Participation Rate

The Q5-based approximations to the federal participation rate were computed pursuant to discussions with staff at CDSS and reflect their suggestions about how to approximate the official federal rates from the Q5 data. The official rates are 42.2 percent for all families and 54.3 percent for two-parent families. This approximation yields estimates of 42.4 and 54.2. Imposing a more natural interpretation of the federal regulations yields slightly lower estimates, 40.1 and 53.6.

Specifically, in our approximation, all cases participating 25 or more hours per week are included in the numerator and the denominator. Unlike the PRWORA requirements shown in Table 2.1, single-parent cases with a child under six years of age that are participating between 20 and 25 hours per week are not considered to participate. Disabled, sanctioned, and caretaker families participating less than 25 hours per week are excluded from the numerator and denominator. Two-parent cases in which either parent is disabled are excluded from the numerator and denominator.

Approximation to the National One-Parent Rate in FFY 1999

The approximation for the nation as a whole is computed using estimates of the shares of cases derived from the FFY 1999 TANF Report to Congress (Tables 2:5.B and 2:6.A). The caseload counts there imply that California's one-parent and two-parent cases are, respectively, 19.7 percent and 4.2 percent of the national total, and the corresponding figures for the balance of the nation are 73.1 percent and 3.1 percent.

Using these weights, we can solve for the all-families rate among one-parent families in the rest of the nation as a function of the all-families rate among two-parent families. Assuming that the all-families rate among two-parent families in the rest of the nation equals the corresponding rate in the nation as a whole yields an estimate for the rest of the nation of 35.7 percent. Taking the weighted average of the one-parent rates for California and the rest of the nation yields the national one-parent rate reported in the text.

The basic conclusion of the text is not very sensitive to the assumption that the all-families rate among two-parent families in the rest of the nation is equal to the rate for California. To see this, note that the all-families rate among two-parent families is bounded from below by the true two-parent rate (i.e., any case that is "participating" according to the two-parent definition is also "participating" according to the all-families definition, and some two-parent cases that are not participating according to the two-parent definition are participating according to the all-families definition). For example, our computations from the Q5 data imply that 54.2 percent of the two-parent cases are participating according to the two-parent definition, but a higher fraction, 63.2 percent, are participating according to the all-families definition.

Similar weighted-average calculations imply that the two-parent rate for the rest of the nation is 55.2 percent, slightly higher than the rate for California (54.3 percent). Thus, the possible range of all-family rates among two-parent cases is between 55.2 percent and 100.0 percent. The implied range of national one-parent rates is only 36.5 percent to 35.0 percent. Given California's all-family rate among two-parent cases of 63.2 percent, and since in the rest of the nation, the all-families rate computed on the two-parent cases is 0.9 percentage points higher than in California, perhaps a better estimate would be 64.1 percent. This value also yields the estimate of 36.0. Over the range 60.0 percent to 70.0 percent, the range of national all-families rates computed on the one-family cases is only 36.1 percent to 35.7 percent.

Bias in the EDD-Based Approximation to Hours Worked

The text imputes full-time work based on earnings greater than the equivalent of full-time work at the minimum wage ($5.75 per hour prior to January 2001). This estimate is only a proxy. The error could be in either direction. There are several issues.

First, these tabulations include only people on aid for all three months of the quarter, because the data do not indicate in which months the work occurred. Someone who came on aid in the third month of the quarter, for example, could have worked prior to being on aid and lost her job, or she could have found a job by going on aid. Employment rates tend to be lower in the quarter in which someone entered aid and higher in the quarter in which they left. However, alternative tabulations including anyone who was on aid even for one month of the quarter are similar.

Second, for individuals with a wage greater than the minimum wage (and the limited available evidence suggests that more than half of working recipients are in this group), the true number of hours worked is lower than our proxy.

Third, this approximation also assumes that hours worked are constant over the three months of the quarter. Someone working only part of the quarter might have worked more than the cutoff number of hours in some months, but not in others. Thus, we may classify some people as working more than the cutoff number of hours in all three months of the quarter when in fact they only worked more than the cutoff number of hours in some of the months. Conversely, some people whom we classify as not working the cutoff number of hours in the quarter may have worked the cutoff number of hours in some of the months.

Fourth, not all employment is covered by the UI system. As noted earlier, those working for the federal government, the self-employed, those in the ambiguous independent contractor category (before 2001), and those working out of state have no earnings shown in the UI data.

This last issue would lead us to expect that UI earnings would be lower than true earnings. Yet UI earnings appear to be higher than earnings reported to the county welfare department (and presumably used in computing benefits) as established by the Q5 manual record check. We also note that this is the federal (DHHS-approved) method for "increasing its actual work participation rate" (letter, M. Howland to S. Fujii, July 6, 1999; see also reply of A. Collins to M. Howland, July 28, 1999). In earlier years, it yielded a higher (by 2.2 percentage points for FFY 1997) estimate of participation rates than did the case files.

Dynamic Decomposition of Caseload Changes and Effects on the Caseload

In Section 3, we analyze the change in the caseload in terms of changes in the underlying flows. This analysis is based on the model in Klerman and Haider

(2001), Haider, Klerman, and Roth (2001), and Haider and Klerman (2001). Those reports provide a more complete discussion of the model.

Briefly, the model includes flows onto aid (the entry rate), flows off aid (the exit rate), and flows back onto aid (the reentry rate). Generically, the flows can be aggregated to simulate changes in the stock using conventional Markov process results:

$$\underset{(Q\times1)}{S_t} = \underset{(Q\times Q)}{M_t(Y_t,\theta)}\ \underset{(Q\times1)}{S_{t-1}}$$

The model we use here (with entry, exit, and reentry, and the assumptions needed to handle the initial-conditions problem) can be represented as

$$
\begin{bmatrix} S(r,1,t) \\ S(r,2,t) \\ S(r,3,t) \\ S(r,4,t) \\ S(o,1,t) \\ S(o,2,t) \\ S(o,3,t) \\ S(o,4,t) \\ S(n,t) \end{bmatrix} =
\begin{bmatrix}
0 & 0 & 0 & 0 & b^1 & b^2 & b^3 & b^4 & e \\
c^1 & 0 & 0 & 0 & 0 & 0 & 0 & 0 & 0 \\
0 & c^2 & 0 & 0 & 0 & 0 & 0 & 0 & 0 \\
0 & 0 & c^3 & c^4 & 0 & 0 & 0 & 0 & 0 \\
1-c^1 & 1-c^2 & 1-c^3 & 1-c^4 & 0 & 0 & 0 & 0 & 0 \\
0 & 0 & 0 & 0 & 1-b^1 & 0 & 0 & 0 & 0 \\
0 & 0 & 0 & 0 & 0 & 1-b^2 & 0 & 0 & 0 \\
0 & 0 & 0 & 0 & 0 & 0 & 1-b^3 & 0 & 0 \\
0 & 0 & 0 & 0 & 0 & 0 & 0 & 1-b^4 & 1-e
\end{bmatrix}
\begin{bmatrix} S(r,1,t-1) \\ S(r,2,t-1) \\ S(r,3,t-1) \\ S(r,4,t-1) \\ S(o,1,t-1) \\ S(o,2,t-1) \\ S(o,3,t-1) \\ S(o,4,t-1) \\ S(n,t-1) \end{bmatrix}
$$

The decompositions into the effects of entry/exit/reentry are done using this model, holding some of the rates fixed at their values at the peak (1995) and allowing the other flows to follow their observed paths.

Table C.1

Classification of Counties by Urbanization

Designation	Counties
Urban	San Francisco, Orange, Alameda, San Mateo, Santa Clara, Contra Costa, Sacramento, San Diego
Mixed	Santa Cruz, Marin, Solano, Ventura, San Joaquin, Stanislaus, Sonoma, Riverside, Napa, Yolo, Santa Barbara, Placer, Fresno, Butte, Sutter, Monterey, Merced, Yuba
Rural	Nevada, El Dorado, Kings, San Bernardino, Kern, Tulare, San Luis Obispo, Amador, Madera, Lake, Shasta, Calaveras, Humboldt, Imperial, Del Norte, San Benito, Mendocino, Tuolumne, Glenn, Tehama, Colusa, Mariposa, Plumas, Siskiyou, Lassen, Trinity, Mono, Sierra, Alpine, Inyo, Modoc
Los Angeles	Los Angeles

SOURCE: Based on population per square mile in the 1994 County and City Data Book.

D. Results of the Policy Simulation Conducted on Participation Rates

As noted in Section 2, changes to the benefit structure affect employment among current recipients and participation rates in two different ways. First, there is a behavioral effect: Because a recipient would take home more of her earnings, she works more. Second, there is a mechanical effect. A higher earned-income disregard and a lower BRR imply that a recipient remains eligible for cash assistance at a higher level of total earnings. Under the benefit structure in California, a woman with two children must work full time at about $8.75 an hour to be income-ineligible for CalWORKs. In many other states, full-time or even half-time work at the minimum wage makes a family income-ineligible for cash assistance. Thus, recipients who in another state would be income-ineligible remain eligible for, and often remain on, welfare in California.

Using the Q5 data, we can simulate the magnitude of the effect of benefit structure on the participation rate. Our analysis focuses on those working sufficient hours to be income-ineligible in other states (half-time to full-time at the federal minimum wage, $5.15 per hour). Because they are working more than 25 hours per week, they appear in both the numerator and the denominator of the federal participation rate in California, raising the rate over what it would be in a state with a lower level of maximum earnings. We tabulate the fraction of California welfare cases with earnings high enough to make them income-ineligible in other states. Assuming that every such person was participating according to the federal definition, we can compute the effect on the participation rate.

Table D.1 presents the results of such a simulation. It gives the percentage drop in the caseload that would occur if California adopted the benefit structure of each state (the benefit structures are described in Choesni et al., 2000), as well as the effect on the participation rate.[1]

This simple simulation ignores the behavioral response to the benefit structure. We can use conventional labor-supply models and estimates to make a rough

---

[1]The effect on the participation rate is computed as $P^* = (P - f)/(1 - f)$, where P is the baseline participation rate, f is the fraction of the caseload that would be income-ineligible in the other state, and P^* is the implied participation rate given the other state's benefit structure.

Table D.1

Effect of Benefit Structure on Participation Rates

State	Maximum Earnings ($)	Mechanical Model		Behavioral Model	
		% of Caseload	Participation Rate (%)	% of Caseload	Participation Rate (%)
AL	205	-24.9	23.0	-26.5	21.4
AK	1,641	-0.1	42.1	0.1	42.3
AZ	586	-10.0	35.8	-10.9	35.2
AR	697	-20.8	27.0	-22.0	25.9
CA	1,477	0.0	42.2	0.0	42.2
CO	511	-20.0	27.7	-21.4	26.4
CT	1,157	-1.1	41.6	-1.3	41.5
DE	958	-3.0	40.4	-3.2	40.3
DC	858	-2.4	40.8	-2.8	40.6
FL	806	-6.8	38.0	-7.6	37.4
GA	514	-14.9	32.1	-16.3	30.9
HI	1,363	-0.5	41.9	-0.5	41.9
ID	625	-16.3	30.9	-18.1	29.5
IL	1,131	-4.4	39.6	-4.8	39.3
IN	378	-25.7	22.2	-26.5	21.4
IA	1,065	-0.1	42.2	-0.4	42.0
KS	762	-4.4	39.6	-4.9	39.2
KY	646	-12.7	33.8	-14.1	32.7
LA	310	-23.5	24.4	-24.9	23.0
ME	1,103	0.1	42.3	0.1	42.3
MD	642	-7.7	37.3	-8.2	37.1
MA	1,045	0.2	42.3	0.2	42.3
MI	774	-12.8	33.7	-13.3	33.3
MN	1,400	-8.9	36.6	-8.1	37.1
MS	458	-16.9	30.5	-18.6	29.0
MO	382	-21.2	26.7	-22.6	25.3
MT	824	-12.9	33.7	-13.5	33.2
NE	669	-8.9	36.6	-9.6	36.1
NV	438	-13.4	33.2	-14.3	32.5
NH	1,200	-0.8	41.7	-0.8	41.7
NJ	848	-8.0	37.2	-8.3	37.0
NM	1,028	0.2	42.3	0.2	42.3
NY	1,157	-0.1	42.2	-0.1	42.2
NC	750	-7.5	37.5	-8.6	36.7
ND	1,014	0.1	42.2	0.0	42.2
OH	996	0.1	42.3	0.1	42.2
OK	704	-3.2	40.3	-3.7	40.0
OR	616	-5.8	38.7	-6.1	38.4
PA	806	-6.0	38.5	-6.7	38.1
RI	1,278	0.3	42.4	0.3	42.4
SC	678	-17.2	30.2	-18.4	29.2
SD	628	-10.9	35.1	-11.3	34.9
TN	949	-5.3	38.9	-6.1	38.4
TX	317	-22.9	25.1	-24.5	23.4
UT	1,002	-1.6	41.3	-1.8	41.2
VT	979	-11.6	34.6	-11.6	34.6
VA	1,157	-17.0	30.4	-18.5	29.1
WA	1,092	-3.8	39.9	-3.9	39.8
WV	547	-6.3	38.3	-7.1	37.8
WI	673	-0.6	41.8	-0.6	41.9
WY	540	-23.7	24.2	-23.7	24.3
U.S. Total		-11.3	34.8	-12.6	33.9

NOTES: Maximum earnings are the maximum earnings at which a family of three remains eligible for benefits in the state (see Table A.1). The mechanical model assumes no effect on hours; the behavioral model incorporates the behavioral response according to the method of Ashenfelter (1983). Percent of caseload is the implied drop in California's caseload that would occur with the adoption of each state's benefit structure. Participation rate is the implied participation rate under the assumption that everyone who is dropped participated according to the federal definition.

SOURCE: Based on RAND simulations.

102

correction for such behavioral effects (Ashenfelter, 1983; Blank, Card, and Robbins, 2000). The behavioral responses will, in general, lead to a caseload decline somewhat larger than that resulting from the mechanical response.[2] The behavioral response magnifies the effect, so that, for the example of Alabama, the caseload declines slightly more (26.5 percent) and the participation rate also declines slightly more (to 21.4 percent), as shown in Table D.1.

In contrast to Alabama, which has one of the lowest benefit levels, the impact on California's caseload and on the participation rate are among the largest for any state. The last row of the table presents estimates weighting over all 50 states, where the weights are the caseloads. It suggests that if California were to adopt the "average" benefit structure of other states, its participation rate would be about 5.7 percent lower. Put differently, about 8 percentage points of California's participation rate result from the benefit structure.

_____

[2]The analysis is similar to the conventional analysis of the EITC, in reverse. Cases in California with earnings just above the cutoff in the other state would certainly not collect welfare in the other state, where the benefit level is lower, causing them to work more; and the BRR is lower. (On welfare in California, they faced a 50 percent BRR; off welfare in the other state, they face a 0 BRR.) For these people, the mechanical simulation is exactly correct.

Cases in California with earnings just below the cutoff in the other state would choose either to continue to collect welfare or to work more and stop collecting welfare. The lower benefit induces them to work more, possibly making them income-ineligible; the higher BRR (California's 50 percent rate compared to BRRs of 67 percent or higher) causes them to want to work less. For these cases, the mechanical effect may be too small (in absolute value); the net behavioral effect is a small increase in work, causing some of these recipients (who remained income-eligible according to the mechanical simulation) to become income-ineligible. Therefore, the behavioral model yields a decrease in the caseload and in the participation rate that is larger than that of the mechanical model, but not much larger.

E. Caseload Decline by California Region and County

In Section 3, we discussed the variation in the caseload decline among the regions in California. In Table E.1, we present the detailed results of the decline by both region and individual county.

Table E.1

Caseload Decline by Region and County

			% Change						
County	Caseload 9/2000	% of State	3/90–3/95	3/95–7/96	7/96–7/97	7/97–7/98	7/98–7/99	7/99–7/00	7/00–9/00	From Peak
Statewide	537,908	100.0	42.0	-5.4	-12.0	-12.9	-10.2	-10.0	-1.4	-42.3
North	22,629	4.2	18.7	-4.2	-13.4	-8.9	-10.9	-9.5	-3.4	-41.1
Butte	4,400	0.8	22.4	-0.7	-11.8	-11.0	-9.6	-10.3	-5.2	-40.0
Colusa	186	0.0	38.3	-21.6	-13.0	-19.4	-21.7	-6.0	-0.5	-59.7
Del Norte	740	0.1	25.9	-6.4	-4.6	-10.5	-11.5	-10.1	-3.4	-38.6
Glenn	511	0.1	10.0	-11.0	-13.0	-4.9	-10.5	-5.6	-1.9	-39.0
Humboldt	2,619	0.5	8.8	-9.0	-26.9	11.3	-8.0	-5.8	-3.8	-38.3
Lake	1,786	0.3	26.1	-4.2	-11.5	-2.4	-10.4	-6.4	-0.2	-30.7
Lassen	502	0.1	15.6	-11.3	-10.3	-9.5	-10.0	-17.8	-6.0	-50.0
Mendocino	1,830	0.3	20.4	-8.0	-14.7	-13.0	-8.3	-7.7	2.5	-40.8
Modoc	199	0.0	16.3	1.8	-19.0	-6.1	-16.8	-16.3	-7.4	-50.1
Nevada	519	0.1	31.9	-8.0	-23.1	-9.9	-23.5	-12.3	-4.2	-59.1
Plumas	191	0.0	13.0	-11.9	-11.2	-18.5	10.1	-39.5	-9.5	-61.6
Shasta	3,776	0.7	12.4	3.7	-6.1	-11.7	-14.2	-7.8	-5.1	-35.4
Sierra	24	0.0	-19.4	2.0	-23.5	2.6	-5.0	-15.8	-25.0	-52.0
Siskiyou	860	0.2	21.0	-8.7	-12.2	-21.3	-12.2	-7.9	-4.2	-51.2
Sutter	1,110	0.2	26.0	-10.4	-11.2	-13.9	-7.9	-13.4	-4.8	-48.1
Tehama	1,206	0.2	25.6	0.2	-14.0	-9.6	-12.0	-7.1	-0.7	-36.8
Trinity	239	0.0	14.9	2.1	-23.0	-3.3	-8.4	-13.9	-6.3	-43.8
Yuba	1,931	0.4	16.6	-3.9	-14.8	-8.8	-11.6	-11.3	-1.4	-42.2
Central Valley	122,051	22.7	31.0	-4.3	-10.6	-10.6	-9.8	-10.1	-1.8	-39.1
Alpine	25	0.0	-24.5	18.9	-43.2	-16.0	14.3	4.2	0.0	-32.4
Amador	255	0.0	46.6	-11.8	-3.7	-12.9	-15.4	-9.8	-0.8	-44.1
Calaveras	455	0.1	35.2	-6.4	-6.7	-19.6	-14.8	-13.8	-6.4	-51.7
El Dorado	923	0.2	23.0	-7.5	-18.7	-15.1	-14.7	-20.8	-1.6	-57.5
Fresno	22,054	4.1	18.4	-8.4	-12.2	-7.6	-9.1	-8.7	-2.3	-39.8
Inyo	213	0.0	12.8	-13.0	4.1	-12.6	-19.8	-16.0	-5.3	-49.5
Kern	16,506	3.1	56.1	0.0	-9.6	-11.0	-4.5	-10.9	-1.9	-32.8
Kings	2,233	0.4	34.9	-1.8	-13.7	-16.8	-10.4	-10.1	-2.9	-44.9
Madera	3,055	0.6	50.0	2.6	-6.8	-7.1	-5.1	-7.9	-1.3	-23.4
Mariposa	180	0.0	21.1	-6.6	-4.9	-17.9	-17.5	-18.3	-6.3	-54.0
Merced	6,209	1.2	46.4	-4.1	-12.9	-12.9	-11.0	-8.1	-2.2	-41.8
Mono	44	0.0	63.8	-6.2	-18.9	-7.0	-7.5	-28.4	-17.0	-61.1
Placer	1,306	0.2	37.5	-11.5	-13.7	-20.8	-18.1	-16.1	-1.4	-59.0
Sacramento	30,869	5.7	29.8	-2.9	-8.1	-7.5	-10.6	-9.7	-0.9	-34.0

Table E.1 (continued)

County	Caseload 9/2000	% of State	3/90–3/95	3/95–7/96	7/96–7/97	7/97–7/98	7/98–7/99	7/99–7/00	7/00–9/00	From Peak
						% Change				
San Joaquin	13,145	2.4	20.6	-3.2	-11.3	-11.3	-10.2	-12.4	-2.6	-41.6
San Luis Obispo	1,751	0.3	43.4	-2.5	-12.2	-19.3	-18.7	-12.1	1.2	-50.0
Stanislaus	8,790	1.6	32.8	-5.0	-10.5	-17.2	-13.1	-10.0	-2.5	-46.3
Tulare	10,959	2.0	33.2	-6.6	-11.6	-9.3	-9.7	-8.0	-1.7	-38.9
Tuolumne	823	0.2	28.6	-1.5	-15.5	-12.4	-9.5	-6.9	3.0	-36.7
Yolo	2,256	0.4	23.7	-6.4	-10.4	-15.6	-10.2	-16.7	-3.1	-48.7
Bay Area	62,096	11.5	30.3	-9.3	-15.8	-16.2	-13.5	-17.0	-3.3	-55.5
Alameda	19,423	3.6	23.1	-9.8	-10.5	-11.2	-12.3	-16.0	-2.8	-48.6
Contra Costa	9,150	1.7	21.7	-7.0	-10.4	-12.3	-11.9	-15.2	-2.0	-46.5
Marin	756	0.1	35.6	-10.3	-10.4	-22.1	-13.5	-20.3	-1.3	-57.4
Monterey	4,278	0.8	55.8	-16.1	-15.5	-10.2	-11.8	-12.1	-4.0	-52.6
Napa	488	0.1	24.7	-14.4	-19.2	-24.1	-28.3	-21.6	-0.4	-70.6
San Benito	474	0.1	57.3	2.1	-21.0	-18.1	-12.8	0.6	-12.5	-49.4
San Francisco	5,401	1.0	7.8	-8.5	-16.8	-14.7	-14.2	-21.2	-3.4	-57.5
San Mateo	1,695	0.3	55.1	-14.5	-25.4	-31.5	-25.0	-22.1	-3.9	-75.5
Santa Clara	11,366	2.1	39.9	-8.5	-25.4	-23.0	-12.9	-17.8	-4.2	-64.0
Santa Cruz	1,845	0.3	49.5	-13.8	-13.1	-18.5	-10.7	-14.8	-5.2	-56.0
Solano	4,626	0.9	36.2	-1.7	-8.9	-12.1	-13.2	-20.5	-4.3	-48.0
Sonoma	2,594	0.5	35.5	-9.7	-14.5	-26.8	-21.5	-16.7	-1.0	-63.4
South	118,665	22.1	54.6	-6.4	-13.3	-16.8	-12.9	-13.5	-1.0	-49.6
Imperial	4,140	0.8	55.7	-4.0	-4.0	-12.6	-7.6	-15.3	1.1	-36.3
Orange	19,645	3.7	87.7	-8.8	-17.2	-20.1	-10.8	-10.5	-1.0	-52.3
Riverside	20,423	3.8	62.3	-1.6	-13.0	-15.4	-12.3	-13.8	0.1	-45.2
San Bernardino	36,069	6.7	50.3	-5.9	-11.4	-14.5	-11.6	-10.2	-1.3	-44.2
San Diego	29,167	5.4	40.4	-7.4	-13.8	-18.4	-19.6	-16.7	-2.3	-57.3
Santa Barbara	3,555	0.7	51.3	-11.3	-13.1	-16.4	16.6	-31.7	-0.5	-48.9
Ventura	5,666	1.1	51.9	-8.6	-14.4	-16.7	-11.6	-9.7	1.5	-47.2
Los Angeles	212,467	39.5	50.4	-3.8	-10.3	-11.0	-7.4	-5.6	-0.6	-33.3

SOURCE: County CA 237 submissions.

Bibliography

American Public Human Services Association, "Frequently Asked Questions: What Is a Welfare Waiver?" at http://www.apwa.org/faq/quest5a.htm (accessed December 18, 1998).

Ashenfelter, Orley, "Determining Participation in Income-Tested Social Programs," *Journal of the American Statistical Association*, Vol. 78, No. 383, September 1983.

Assistant Secretary for Planning and Evaluation, "'Leavers' and Diversion Studies: Summary of Research on Welfare Outcomes Funded by ASPE," June 2000, at http://aspe.os.dhhs.gov/hsp/leavers99.

Bane, M., and D. Ellwood, *Welfare Realities: From Rhetoric to Reform*, Cambridge, MA: Harvard University Press, 1994.

Becerra, Rosina M., Alisa Lewin, Michael N. Mitchell, and Hiromi Ono, *California Work Pays Demonstration Project: Report on First Thirty Months*, Los Angeles, CA: UCLA School of Public Policy and Social Research, Welfare Policy Research Group, 1996, at http://ucdata.berkeley.edu/CWPDP/execsum.PDF.

Becerra, Rosina M., Alisa Lewin, Michael N. Mitchell, and Hiromi Ono, *California Work Pays Demonstration Project: Report on First Forty-Two Months*, Los Angeles, CA: UCLA School of Public Policy and Social Research, Welfare Policy Research Group, 1998.

Bell, Stephen, "New Federalism and Research: Rearranging Old Methods to Study New Social Policies in the States," Washington, D.C.: The Urban Institute, August, 1999, at http://newfederalism.urban.org/html/discussion99-08.html.

Berlin, Gordon L., "Encouraging Work, Reducing Poverty: The Impact of Work Incentive Programs," New York: Manpower Demonstration Research Corporation (MDRC), March 2000, at http://www.mdrc.org/Reports2000/EWORK-RPOVERTY.pdf or http://frontpage.mdrc.aa.psiweb.com/Reports2000/EWORK-RPOVERTY.pdf.

Berlin, Gordon L., "Welfare That Works," *The American Prospect*, Vol. 11, No. 15, June 19–July 3, 2000, at http://www.prospect.org/archives/V11-15/berlin.html.

Bishop, John H., "Is Welfare Reform Succeeding?" Ithaca, NY: Cornell University, Working Paper, 1998.

Blank, Rebecca M., "Fighting Poverty: Lessons from Recent U.S. History," *Journal of Economic Perspectives*, Vol. 14, No. 2, Spring 2000, pp. 3–19.

Blank, Rebecca M., "Policy Watch: The 1996 Welfare Reform," *Journal of Economic Perspectives*, Vol. 11, No. 1, Winter 1997, pp. 169–177.

Blank, Rebecca M., "The Effect of Medical Need and Medicaid on AFDC Participation," *Journal of Human Resources*, Vol. 24, No. 1, 1989, pp. 54–87.

Blank, Rebecca M., "What Causes Public Assistance Caseloads to Grow?," *Journal of Human Resources*, Vol. 36, No. 1, Winter 2001.

Blank, Rebecca M., David Card, and Philip K. Robbins, "Financial Incentives for Increasing Work and Income Among Low-Income Families," Cambridge, MA: National Bureau of Economic Research, Working Paper #6998, March 1999, at http://papers.nber.org/papers/W6998.

Blank, Rebecca M., David Card, and Philip K. Robbins, "Financial Incentives for Increasing Work and Income Among Low-Income Families," in Rebecca M. Blank and David Card (eds.), *Finding Jobs: Work and Welfare Reform*, New York, NY: Russell Sage Foundation, 2000.

Bloom, Dan, *ReWORKing Welfare Series After AFDC: Welfare-to-Work Choices and Challenges for States*, New York: Manpower Demonstration Research Corporation, 1997.

Bloom, Dan, *Welfare Time Limits: An Interim Report*, New York: Manpower Demonstration Research Corporation, April 1999, at http://www.mdrc.org/Reports99/CrossState/CrossStateFull.html.

Bloom, Dan, Laura Melton, Charles Michalopoulos, Susan Scrivener, and Johanna Walter, *Jobs First: Implementation and Early Impacts of Connecticut's Welfare Reform Initiative*, New York: Manpower Demonstration Research Corporation, 2000.

Bloom, Dan, Charles Michalopoulos, Johanna Walter, and Patricia Auspos, *Implementation and Early Impacts of Vermont's Welfare Restructuring Project*, New York: Manpower Demonstration Research Corporation, 1998.

Bloom, Dan, and LaDonna Pavetti, *Sanctions and Time Limits: State Policies, Their Implementation, and Outcomes for Families*, conference paper prepared for "The New World of Welfare: Shaping a Post-TANF Agenda for Policy," Washington, D.C., February 1–2, 2001.

Brady, Henry E., and Barbara West Snow, "Data Systems and Statistical Requirements for the Personal Responsibility and Work Opportunity Act of 1996," paper prepared for National Academy of Sciences, October 14, 1999.

Brauner, Sarah, and Pamela Loprest, "Where Are They Now? What States' Studies of People Who Left Welfare Tell Us," Series A, No. A-32, *New Federalism, Issues and Options for States*, Washington, D.C.: The Urban Institute, May 1999.

Brown, Amy, *Work First: How to Implement an Employment-Focused Approach to Welfare Reform*, New York: Manpower Demonstration Research Corporation, 1997, at http://www.mdrc.org/Reports/workfirst.htm.

Brown, Amy, Dan Bloom, and David Butler, *The View from the Field: As Time Limits Approach, Welfare Recipients and Staff Talk About Their Attitudes and Expectations*, New York: Manpower Demonstration Research Corporation, 1997.

Burtless, G., "The Case for Randomized Field Trials in Economic and Policy Research," *Journal of Economic Perspectives*, Vol. 9, No. 2 (Spring), pp. 63–84, 1995.

California Budget Project, "How Can Federal Welfare-to-Work Grants Help Move Californians from Welfare to Work?" Budget Brief, November 1997, at http://www.cbp.org/brief/bb971102.html.

California Budget Project, *Making Ends Meet: How Much Does It Cost To Raise A Family In California?* October 1999.

California Budget Project, "Welfare Reform and Funding Choices: What Does the TANF Maintenance of Effort Requirement Mean for California?", Budget Brief, December 1998, at http://www.cbp.org/brief/bb981201.html.

California Budget Project, "CalWORKs: What Do We Know Two Years Later?", Welfare Reform Update, April 2000.

Cancian, Maria, Robert Haveman, Thomas Kaplan, Daniel Meyer, and Barbara Wolfe, "Work, Earnings, and Well-Being After Welfare: What Do We Know?," *Focus*, Vol. 20, No. 2, 1999, pp. 22–25.

Card, David, "Using Regional Variation in Wages to Measure the Effects of the Federal Minimum Wage," *Industrial and Labor Relations Review*, Vol. 46, No. 1, 1992, pp. 22–37.

Casper, Lynne, "Who's Minding Our Preschoolers," *Current Population Reports*, Washington, D.C.: U.S. Department of Commerce, March 1996.

Center on Budget and Policy Priorities, "The TANF Block Grant Should Not Be Cut," Washington, D.C., March 11, 1999, at http://www.cbpp.org/3-11-99wel.htm.

Clinton, William J., statement at signing of the Personal Responsibility and Work Opportunity Reconciliation Act of 1996, The White House, August 20, 1996.

Corbett, Thomas, "Changing the Culture of Welfare," *Focus*, 16:2, Winter 1994–95, at http://www.ssc.wisc.edu/irp/pubs/focusold/16.2.a/changing.txt.

Corcoran, Mary, and Susanna Loeb, "Will Wages Grow With Experience for Welfare Mothers?" *Focus*, Vol. 20, No. 2, 1999, pp. 20–21.

Council of Economic Advisers, *Explaining the Decline in Welfare Receipt, 1993–1996*, Washington, D.C., May 9, 1997, at http://www.whitehouse.gov/WH/EOP/CEA/Welfare/Technical_Report.html.

Council of Economic Advisers, *Economic Expansion, Welfare Reform, and the Decline in Welfare Caseloads: An Update* (Technical Report), Washington, D.C., August 1999.

Council of Economic Advisers, *The Effects of Welfare Policy and the Economic Expansion on Welfare Caseloads: An Update*, A Report of the Council of Economic Advisers, August 3, 1999.

Council of Economic Advisers, *The Effects of Welfare Policy and the Economic Expansion on Welfare Caseloads: An Update*, at http://www.whitehouse.gov/WH/EOP/CEA/html/welfare.

Cox, Amy G., Nicole Humphrey, and Jacob A. Klerman, *Welfare Reform in California: Results of the 1999 CalWORKs Program Staff Survey*, Santa Monica, CA: RAND, MR-1181.0-CDSS, 2001.

Currie, Janet and Aaron Yelowitz, "Health Insurance and Less Skilled Workers," Working Paper, UCLA, 1998.

Cutler, David M. and Jonathan Gruber, "Does Public Insurance Crowd our Private Insurance," *Quarterly Journal of Economics*, Vol. 112, No. 2, May 1996, pp. 391–430.

Danziger, Sheldon, Robert Haveman, and Robert Plotnick, "How Income Transfers Affect Work, Savings, and the Income Distribution: A Critical Review," *Journal of Economic Literature*, Vol. 19, 1981, pp. 975–1028.

"Day Care Operators Find Welfare Reform 'Nightmare,'" *Sacramento Bee*, August 19, 1999.

Dehejia, R., and S. Wahba, "Causal Effects in Non-Experimental Studies: Re-Evaluating the Evaluation of Training Programs," *Journal of the American Statistical Association*, Vol. 94, No. 448, 1999, pp. 1053–1062.

DeParle, Jason, "As Benefits Expire, the Experts Worry," *New York Times*, October 10, 1999.

DeParle, Jason, "States Struggle to Use Windfall Born of Shifts in Welfare Law," *New York Times*, August 18, 1999.

Dertouzos, Jim, and Patricia A. Ebener, *1999 San Bernardino Health and Social Services Survey Report: Work in Progress Presentation*, 2000.

Dickens, William, "Error Components in Grouped Data Is It Ever Worth Weighting?" *Review of Economics and Statistics*, 1990, pp. 328–333.

Dickert, Stacy, Scott Houser, and John Karl Scholz, "The Earned Income Tax Credit and Transfer Programs: A Study of Labor Market and Program Participation," in *Tax Policy and the Economy 9*, James M. Poterba, ed., Cambridge, MA: MIT Press, 1995, pp. 1–50.

Ebener, Patricia A., and Jacob A. Klerman, *Welfare Reform in California: Results of the 1998 All-County Implementation Survey*, Santa Monica, CA: RAND, MR-1052-CDSS, 1999.

Ebener, Patricia A., and Jacob A. Klerman, *Welfare Reform in California: Results of the 1999 All-County Implementation Survey*, Santa Monica, CA: RAND, MR-1180-CDSS, 2001.

Ebener, Patricia A., Elizabeth A. Roth, and Jacob A. Klerman, *Welfare Reform in California: Appendix: Results of the 1998 All-County Implementation Survey*, Santa Monica, CA: RAND, MR-1052/1-CDSS, 1999.

Edelman, P., "The Worst Thing Bill Clinton Has Done," *The Atlantic Monthly*, March 1997.

Edin, Kathryn, and Laura Lein, *Making Ends Meet: How Single Mothers Survive Welfare and Low-Wage Work*, New York: Russell Sage Foundation, 1997.

Eissa, Nada, and Hilary Williamson Hoynes *The Earned Income Tax Credit and the Labor Supply of Married Couples*, Cambridge, MA: National Bureau of Economic Research, Working Paper #6856, 1998.

Eissa, Nada, and Hilary Williamson Hoynes, "Good News for Low Income Families? Tax Transfer Schemes and Marriage," Mimeo, Berkeley, CA: University of California, 1999.

Eissa, Nada, and Jeffrey B. Liebman, "Labor Supply Response to the Earned Income Tax Credit," *Quarterly Journal of Economics*, Vol. 111, No. 2, 1995, pp. 605–37.

Ellis, Virginia, "State Fails to Meet U.S. Welfare-to-Work Goal," *Los Angeles Times*, January 25, 1999, p. A-1.

Ellis, Virginia, "State Kills Project to Link Welfare Networks," *Los Angeles Times*, July 12, 1999.

Ellwood, David T., "The Impact of the EITC on Work and Social Policy Reforms on Work, Marriage, and Living Arrangements," Mimeo, Cambridge, MA: Kennedy School of Government, November 1999.

Ellwood, Deborah A., "Welfare Reform as I Knew It: When Bad Things Happen to Good Policies," *The American Prospect*, May–June 1996 at http://epn.org/prospect/26/26ellw.html (accessed January 26, 1999).

Ellwood, Deborah A., and Donald J. Boyd, "Changes in State Spending on Social Services Since the Implementation of Welfare Reform: A Preliminary Report," Albany, NY: The Nelson A. Rockefeller Institute of Government, February 2000.

Fein, David, and Jennifer Karweit, *The ABC Evaluation: The Early Economic Impacts of Delaware's A Better Chance Welfare Reform Program*, Cambridge, MA: Abt Associates Inc., 1997.

Fernandez, Nuria, Deputy Administrator, US FTA, Address to the American Public Transit Association Meeting, September 23, 1997.

Figlio, David N., and James P. Ziliak, "Welfare Reform, the Business Cycle, and the Decline in AFDC Caseloads," in Sheldon Danziger (ed.), *Economic Conditions and Welfare Reform*, Kalamazoo, MI: W.E. Upjohn Institute, 1999.

Fischer, Will, Emilie Neumann, and Cheryl Waldrip. "CalWORKs Orientations: Analysis of Orientation Attendance and Recommendations for Improvement," Berkeley, CA: Alameda County Social Services Agency, October 1998.

Freedman, Stephen, Daniel Friedlander, Gayle Hamilton, JoAnn Rock, Marisa Mitchell, Jodi Nudelman, Amanda Schweder, and Laura Storto, *Evaluating Alternative Welfare-to-Work Approaches: Two-Year Impacts for Eleven Programs*, National Evaluation of Welfare-to-Work Strategies, Washington, D.C.: U.S. Department of Health and Human Services, Administration for Children and Families and Office of the Assistant Secretary for Planning and Evaluation; and U.S. Department of Education, Office of the Under Secretary and Office of Vocational and Adult Education, 1999.

Freedman, Stephen, Daniel Friedlander, Winston Lin, and Amanda Schweder, "Five-Year Impacts on Employment, Earnings, and AFDC Receipt," New York: Manpower Demonstration Research Corporation, GAIN Evaluation Working Paper 96.1, July 1996.

Freedman, Stephen, Jean Knab, Lisa Gennetian, and David Navarro, *The Los Angeles Jobs-First GAIN Evaluation: Final Report on a Work First Program in a Major Urban Center*, New York: Manpower Demonstration Research Corporation, June 2000, at http://www.mdrc.org/Reports2000/LA-GAIN/LA-GAIN-FullReport.pdf.

Freedman, Stephen, Marisa Mitchell, and David Navarro, "The Los Angeles Jobs-First GAIN Evaluation: Preliminary Findings on Participation Patterns and First Year Impacts," New York: Manpower Demonstration Research Corporation, Working Paper, August 1998.

Friedlander, Daniel, David H. Greenberg, and Philip K. Robbins, "Evaluating Government Training Programs for the Economically Disadvantaged," *Journal of Economic Literature*, Vol. 35, No. 4, December 1999, pp. 1809–1855.

"FY1998 TANF Work Participation Rates," August 3, 1999, at http://www.acf.dhhs.gov/news/98table.htm.

Gais, Thomas L., Richard P. Nathan, Irene Lurie, and Thomas Kaplan, *The Implementation of the Personal Responsibility Act of 1996: Commonalities, Variations, and the Challenges of Complexity*, conference paper prepared for "The New World of Welfare: Shaping a Post-TANF Agenda for Policy," Washington, D.C., February 1–2, 2001.

Gallagher, L. J., et al., *One Year After Federal Welfare Reform: A Description of State Temporary Assistance for Needy Families (TANF) Decisions as of October 1997*, Washington, D.C.: The Urban Institute, May 1998.

Garfinkel, I., and S. McLanahan, *Single Mothers and Their Children a New American Dilemma*, Changing Domestic Priorities Series, Washington, D.C.: Urban Institute Press, 1986.

Garrett, Bowen, and John Holahan, "Welfare Leavers, Medicaid Coverage, and Private Health Insurance," Series B, No. B-13, *New Federalism, National Survey of America's Families*, Washington, D.C.: The Urban Institute, March 2000.

Geen, R., W. Zimmerman, T. Douglas, S. Zedlewski, and S. Waters, *Income Support and Social Services for Low-Income People in California*, State Reports Series, Washington, D.C.: The Urban Institute, 1997.

Gingrich, Newt (ed.), Bob Schellhas (ed.), Ed Gillespie, and Dick Armey, *Contract With America: The Bold Plan by Rep. Newt Gingrich, Rep. Dick Armey and the House Republicans to Change the Nation*, New York: Times Books, 1994.

Gladden, Tricia, and Christopher Taber, "Wage Progression Among Less Skilled Workers," in David Card and Rebecca Blank (eds), *Finding Jobs: Work and Welfare Reform*, New York: Russell Sage Foundation, 2000, pp. 160–192.

Goggin, M., *Policy Design and the Politics of Implementation: The Case of Child Health Policy in the American States*, Knoxville, TN: University of Tennessee Press, 1987.

Goggin, M., A. Bowman, J. Lester, and L. O'Toole, *Implementation Theory and Practice: Toward a Third Generation*, Glenview, IL: Scott, Foresman/Little, Brown, 1990.

Goldberg, Heidi, and Liz Schott, *A Compliance-Oriented Approach to Sanctions in State and County TANF Programs*, Washington, D.C.: Center for Budget and Policy Priorities, 2000.

Gordon, Anne, and Roberto Agodini, *Early Impacts of the Virginia Independence Program: Final Report*, Princeton, NJ: Mathematica Policy Research Inc., 1999.

Grant, Bridget, and Deborah Dawson, "Alcohol and Drug Use, Abuse and Dependence Among Welfare Recipients," *American Journal of Public Health*, Vol. 86, No. 10, October 1996.

Greenberg, Mark H., *Beyond Welfare: New Opportunities to Use TANF to Help Low-Income Working Families*, Washington, D.C.: Center for Law and Social Policy, July 1999, at http://www.clasp.org/pubs/TANF/markKELLOGG.PDF.

Greenberg, Mark H., *The TANF Maintenance of Effort Requirement*, Washington, D.C.: Center for Law and Social Policy, December 2000, at http://www.clasp.org/TANF/moe.htm.

Greenberg, Mark H., and Steve Savner, *The Final TANF Regulations: A Preliminary Analysis*, Washington, D.C.: Center for Law and Social Policy, May 1999, at http://www.clasp.org/pubs/TANF/finalregs.html.

Grogger, Jeff, *Time Limits and Welfare Use*, Cambridge, MA: National Bureau of Economic Research, Working Paper 7709, May 2000.

Grogger, Jeff, and Charles Michalopoulos, *Welfare Dynamics under Time Limits*, Cambridge, MA: National Bureau of Economic Research, Working Paper 7353, 1999.

Gueron, Judith M., and Edward Pauly, *From Welfare to Work*, New York: Russell Sage Foundation, 1991.

Haider, Steven, and Jacob Klerman, "Dynamic Properties of the Welfare Caseload," Santa Monica, CA: RAND, unpublished manuscript, 2001.

Haider, Steven, Jacob A. Klerman, Jan M. Hanley, Laurie McDonald, Elizabeth Roth, Liisa Hiatt, and Marika Suttorp, *Welfare Reform in California: Design of the Impact Analysis, Preliminary Investigations of Caseload Data,* Santa Monica, CA: RAND, MR-1086/1 CDSS, 2000.

Haider, Steven, Jacob Klerman, and Elizabeth Roth, "The Relationship Between the Economy and the Welfare Caseload: A dynamic Approach," Santa Monica, CA: RAND, unpublished manuscript, 2001.

Hamilton, Gayle, Thomas Brock, Mary Farrell, Daniel Friedlander, and Kristen Harkenett, The National Evaluation of Welfare-to-Work Strategies: Evaluating Two Welfare-to-Work Program Approaches, Two-Year Findings on the Labor Force Attachment and Human Capital Development Programs in Three Sites, Washington, D.C.: U.S. Department of Health and Human Services, Administration for Children and Families, Office of the Assistance Secretary of Planning and Evaluation, and U.S. Department of Education, Office of the Under Secretary, Office of Vocational and Adult Education, December 1997, at http://www.mdrc.org/Reports/JOBS2Approaches/ JOBS2ApproachesExSum.html.

Hamilton, Gayle, and Susan Scrivener, *Promoting Participation: How to Increase Involvement in Welfare-to-Work Activities,* New York: Manpower Demonstration Research Corporation, September 1999, at http://www.mdrc. org/Reports99/PromotingParticipation.pdf.

Harris, Scott, "Row With State Threatens County Workfare Project," *Los Angeles Times,* September 23, 1998, p. 3.

Haskins, Ron, "Welfare in a Society of Permanent Work," Washington, D.C.: Committee on Ways and Means, unpublished manuscript, 1999, at http:// jcpr.org/wp/Wpprofile.cfm?ID=149.

Haskins, Ron, Isabel Sawhill, and Kent Weaver, "Welfare Reform Reauthorization: An Overview of Problems and Issues," WR&B Policy Brief #2, January 2001.

Haveman, Robert, and Jonathan Schwabish, "Macroeconomic Performance and the Poverty Rate: A Return to Normalcy?" unpublished manuscript, 1998.

Heckman, James, and V. Joseph Hotz, "Choosing Among Alternative Nonexperimental Methods for Estimating the Impact of Social Programs: The Case of Manpower Training," *Journal of the American Statistical Association,* Vol. 84, No. 408, pp. 862–880, 1989.

Heckman, James J., H. Ichimura, and P. Todd, "Matching as an Econometric Evaluation Estimator: Evidence from Evaluating a Job Training Program," *Review of Economic Studies,* Vol. 64, 1997, pp. 605–654.

Heckman, James J., H. Ichimura, and P. Todd, "Matching as an Econometric Evaluation Estimator," *Review of Economic Studies,* Vol. 65, 1998a, pp. 261–294.

Heckman, James J., H. Ichimura, J. Smith, and P. Todd, "Characterizing Selection Bias Using Experimental Data," *Econometrica*, Vol. 66, 1998b, pp. 1017–1098.

Heckman, James J., and Jeffrey A. Smith, "Assessing the Case for Social Experiments," *The Journal of Economic Perspectives*, Vol. 9, No. 2 Spring 1995, pp. 85–110.

Hernandez, Raymond, "Surplus Puts New York at Center of a Debate," *New York Times*, August 19, 1999.

Hill, Elizabeth G., *California Meets Federal Work Participation Rates for CalWORKs in 1998*, Sacramento, CA: Legislative Analysts Office, August 31, 1999b.

Hill, Elizabeth G., *CalWORKs Community Service: What Does It Mean for California?*, Sacramento, CA: Legislative Analysts Office, February 4, 1999a.

Hofferth, Sandra L., Stephen Stanhope, and Kathleen Mullan Harris, "Exiting Welfare in the 1990s: Did Public Policy Influence Recipients' Behavior," unpublished paper, 2000.

Hong, Peter Y., "Welfare Fraud Tab May Hit $500 Million a Year," *Los Angeles Times*, July 1, 1999, p. B-1.

Hotz, V. Joseph, and J. K. Scholz, "Measuring Employment and Income Outcomes for Low-Income Populations with Administrative and Survey Data," Los Angeles, CA: UCLA, unpublished manuscript, 1999.

Hotz, V. Joseph, and J. K. Scholz, "The Earned Income Credit," Los Angeles, CA: UCLA, unpublished manuscript, July 2000, at http://www.econ.ucla.edu/hotz/working_papers/EITC_survey.pdf.

Hotz, V. Joseph, C. Hill, C. Mullin, and J. K. Scholz, *EITC Eligibility, Participation and Compliance Rates for AFDC Households: Evidence from the California Caseload*, Los Angeles, CA: UCLA, April 1999.

Hotz, V. Joseph, Robert Goerge, Julie Balzekas, and Francis Margolin (eds.), *Administrative Data for Policy-Relevant Research: Assessment of Current Utility and Recommendations for Development*, A Report of the Advisory Panel on Research Uses of Administrative Data of the Northwestern University/University of Chicago Joint Center for Poverty Research, January 1998.

Hotz, V. Joseph, Guido Imbens, and Jacob A. Klerman, "The Long-Term Gains from GAIN: A Re-Analysis of the Impacts of the California GAIN Program," unpublished manuscript, Santa Monica, CA: RAND, 2000.

Hotz, V. Joseph, Guido Imbens, and J. Mortimer, "Predicting the Efficacy of Future Training Programs Using Past Experiences," Cambridge, MA: National Bureau of Economic Research, Working Paper No. T0238, April 1999.

Howard, Craig, as quoted in Joan Walsh, "The High Cost of Good Intentions," *San Francisco Examiner Magazine*, November 15, 1998, pp. 10–32.

Hoynes, Hilary, "Work and Marriage Incentives to Welfare Programs: What Have We Learned?," in Alan J. Auerbach (ed.), *Fiscal Policy: Lessons from Economic Research*, Cambridge, MA: MIT Press, 1997.

Hubert, Cynthia, "Non-Paying Jobs Ahead For Many CalWORKs Clients," *Sacramento Bee*, December 17, 1999.

Ifill, Gwen, "Clinton's Plan to 'End Welfare as We Know It': He Proposes Billions for Training and Tax Credits," *The San Francisco Chronicle*, September 10, 1992, p. A1.

"Implementing CalWORKs: Creating a Seamless Systems of Supportive Services, Moving from Welfare to Work," An ADP Forum Sponsored by the California Department of Alcohol and Drug Programs, November 15, 1999.

Johnson, Pamela J., "Adults on Welfare Decrease by Half in 4 Years," *Los Angeles Times*, Ventura County Edition, January 13, 1999, p. B-1.

Klerman, Jacob Alex, *The Pace of CW Implementation*, Santa Monica, CA: RAND, CT-166, 2000.

Klerman, Jacob, and Steven Haider, "A Stock-Flow Analysis of the Welfare Caseload: Insights from California Economic Conditions," Santa Monica, CA: RAND, unpublished manuscript, March 2001.

Klerman, Jacob A., V. Joseph Hotz, Guido Imbens, Paul Steinberg, Elaine Reardon, Patricia A. Ebener, Jennifer Hawes-Dawson, *Welfare Reform in California: Design of the Impact Analysis*, Santa Monica, CA: RAND, MR-1266.0-CDSS, 2000.

Klerman, Jacob A., V. Joseph Hotz, Guido Imbens, Paul Steinberg, Elaine Reardon, Patricia A. Ebener, and Jennifer A. Hawes-Dawson, *Welfare Reform in California: Design of the Impact Analysis*. Santa Monica, CA: RAND, MR-1086-CDSS, October 1999.

Klerman, Jacob A., Elaine Reardon, and Paul S. Steinberg, *RAND Statewide CalWORKs Evaluation: An Overview*. Santa Monica, CA: RAND, DB-252-CDSS, 1998.

Klerman, Jacob A., Gail L. Zellman, and Paul S. Steinberg, *Welfare Reform in California: State and County Implementation of CalWORKs in the Second Year-Executive Summary*, Santa Monica, CA: RAND, MR-1177/1-CDSS, 2001.

Klerman, Jacob A., Gail L. Zellman, Tammi Chun, Nicole Humphrey, Elaine Reardon, Donna Farley, Patricia A. Ebener, and Paul Steinberg, *Welfare Reform in California: State and County Implementation of CalWORKs in the Second Year*, Santa Monica, CA: RAND, MR-1177-CDSS, 2001.

Kondo, Annette, "Suit Planned over Welfare-to-Work Program," *Los Angeles Times*, December 16, 1999.

Kornfeld, R., and H. S. Bloom, "Measuring Program Impacts on Earnings and Employment: Do UI Wage Reports from Employers Agree with Surveys of

Individuals?" *Journal of Labor Economics*, Vol. 17, No. 1, January 1999, pp. 168–197.

Kucher, Karen, "Lawsuit Targets Welfare Contracts: Groups Claim Profit Motivated Awards," *San Diego Union-Tribune*, August 3, 1999, p. B3.

LaLonde, R., "Evaluating the Econometric Evaluations of Training Programs with Experimental Data," *American Economic Review*, Vol. 76, No. 4, 1986, pp. 604–620.

Lazere, Ed, *Allocation of the $3 Billion TANF Rescission Among States Would Treat Some States Inequitably*, Washington, D.C.: Center on Budget and Policy Priorities, September 27, 1999, at http://www.cbpp.org/9-27-99wel.htm.

Lazere, Ed, *Unspent TANF Funds in the Middle of Federal Fiscal Year 2000*, Washington, D.C.: Center on Budget and Policy Priorities, August 2, 2000.

Lazere, Ed, *Welfare Balances After Three Years of TANF Block Grants*, Washington, D.C.: Center on Budget and Policy Priorities, January 12, 2000.

Lazere, Ed, *Welfare Balances After Three Years of TANF Block Grants: Unspent TANF Funds at the End of Federal Fiscal Year 1999*, Washington, D.C.: Center on Budget and Policy Priorities, January 12, 2000.

Lazere, Ed, and Robert Greenstein, *Should TANF Block Grant Funds Be Rescinded?*, Washington, D.C.: Center on Budget and Policy Priorities, September 27, 1999, at http://www.cbpp.org/9-23-99wel.htm.

Legislative Analyst's Office, *Analysis of the 2000-01 Budget Bill Department of Social Services CalWORKs Program (5180)*, at http://www.lao.ca.gov/analysis_2000/health_ss/hss_17_CalWORKs_5180_an100.htm.

Legislative Analyst's Office, *Analysis of Proposition 210*, at http://vote96.ss.ca.gov/Vote96/html/BP/210analysis.htm.

Legislative Analyst's Office, *Federal Welfare Reform (H.R. 3734): Fiscal Effect on California*, Policy Brief, August 20, 1996.

Legislative Analyst's Office, *H.R. 2015, Welfare-to-Work Program Fiscal Overview*, November 17, 1997.

Legislative Analyst's Office, *CalWORKs Welfare Reform: Major Provisions and Issues*, January 23, 1998, at http://www.lao.ca.gov/012398%5Fcalworks.htm.

Legislative Analyst's Office, *Substance Abuse Treatment in California*, July 13, 1999.

Legislative Analyst's Office, *Budget and Policy Implications: California Meets Federal Work Participation Rates for CalWORKs in 1998*, August 31, 1999.

Leung, Shirley, and Sheila Muto, "As `Living Wage' Gains Momentum, A Look at How It Has Done So Far," *Wall Street Journal*, December 15, 1999.

Levin, M., and B. Ferman, "The Political Hand: Policy Implementations and Youth Employment Programs," *Journal of Policy Analysis and Management*, Vol. 5, No. 2, 1986, pp. 311–325.

Levine, Phillip B., and Diane M. Whitmore, "The Impact of Welfare Reform on the AFDC Caseload," Washington, D.C.: National Tax Association, Proceedings, Ninetieth Annual Conference, 1998.

Liebman, Jeffrey B., "The Impact of the Earned Income Tax Credit on Incentives and Income Distribution," in *Tax Policy and the Economy*, 1998.

Loprest, Pamela, "How Families That Left Welfare Are Doing: A National Picture," Series B, No. B-1, *New Federalism, National Survey of America's Families*, Washington, D.C.: The Urban Institute, August 1999.

MaCurdy, Thomas, David Mancuso, and Margaret O'Brien-Strain, *The Rise and Fall of California's Welfare Caseload: Types and Regions, 1980–1999*, San Francisco, CA: Public Policy Institute of California, 2000.

"Making Ends Meet: How Much Does It Cost to Raise a Family in California?", California Budget Project, November 1999, at http://www.cbp.org/reports/r9911mem.html.

Martinson, Karin, and Daniel Friedlander, *GAIN: Basic Education in a Welfare-to-Work Program*, New York: Manpower Demonstration Research Corporation, 1994.

Matthews, Jon, "Workfare Facing Growing Pains," *Sacramento Bee*, 4/10/1989, p. A. 1.

Maxwell, Terrence A., "Welfare Reform and Information Management: Rewiring the Human Service System", Rockefeller Reports, Albany, NY: SUNY Albany, December 5, 1997.

Mazmanian, D., and P. Sabatier (eds.), *Effective Policy Implementation*, Lexington, MA: D.C. Heath, 1983.

McLaughlin, M., "Learning from Experience: Lessons from Policy Implementation," *Educational Evaluation and Policy Analysis*, Vol. 9, No. 2, pp. 171–178.

Mead, Lawrence M., "Expectations and Welfare Work: WIN in New York State," *Polity*, Vol. 18, No. 2, Winter 1985, pp. 224–252.

Mead, Lawrence M., "Optimizing JOBS: Evaluation versus Administration," *Public Administration Review*, Vol. 57, No. 2, March/April 1997, pp. 113–123.

Mead, Lawrence M., "Governmental Quality and Welfare Reform," paper presented at the 2000 Annual Meeting of the American Political Science Association, Marriott Wardman Park, Washington, D.C., August 31–September 3, 2000.

Mena, Jennifer, "Orange County Leads Region in Welfare Roll Decline; Economy Credited," *Los Angeles Times*, Orange County Edition, November 15, 1999, p. B-1.

Mermin, Gordon, and C. Eugene Steuerle, *The Impact of TANF on State Budgets*, Washington, D.C.: The Urban Institute, Policy Brief A-18, November 1997.

Meyer, Bruce, "Natural and Quasi-Experiments in Economics," *Journal of Business and Economic Statistics*, Vol. 13, No. 2, April 1995, pp. 151–161.

Meyer, Bruce D., and Dan T. Rosenbaum, "Welfare, the Earned Income Tax Credit, and the Labor Supply of Single Mothers," Cambridge, MA: National Bureau of Economic Research, Working Paper No. W7363, September 1999.

Meyer, Bruce D., and Dan T. Rosenbaum, "Making Single Mothers Work: Recent Tax and Welfare Policy and Its Effects," Cambridge, MA: National Bureau of Economic Research, Working Paper No. W7491, January 2000.

Meyers, Marcia K., Bonnie Glaser, and Karin MacDonald, "On the Front Lines of Welfare Delivery: Are Workers Implementing Policy Reforms?", *Journal of Policy Analysis and Management*, Vol. 17, No. 1, 1998, pp. 1–22.

Michalopoulos, Charles, Philip K. Robbins, and David Card, "When Financial Incentives Pay for Themselves: Early Findings from the Self-Sufficiency Project's Applicant Study," Chicago, IL: Joint Center for Policy Research, Working Paper 133, January 1, 2000, at http://www.jcpr.org/wpfiles/Michalopoulos_WP.pdf.

Miller, Cynthia, Virginia Knox, Patricia Auspos, Jo Anna Hunter-Manns, and Alan Orenstein, *Making Welfare Work and Work Pay: Implementation and 18-Month Impacts of the Minnesota Family Investment Program*, New York: Manpower Demonstration Research Corporation, 1997.

Mistrano, Sam, "Perspective on Welfare: Welfare Clock Will Run Out Before Job Supply Catches Up," *Los Angeles Times*, July 16, 1999, p. B-7.

Moffitt, Robert A., "Evaluation Methods for Program Entry Effects," in Charles F. Manski and Irwin Garfinkel (eds.), *Evaluating Welfare and Training Programs*, Cambridge, MA: Harvard University Press, 1992b.

Moffitt, Robert A., "Incentive Effects of the U.S. Welfare System," *Journal of Economic Literature*, Vol. 30, No. 1, March 1992a, pp. 1–61.

Moffitt, Robert A., "The Effect of Pre-PRWORA Waivers on AFDC Caseloads and Female Earnings, Income, and Labor Force Behavior," Chicago, IL: Joint Center for Policy Research, Working Paper 89.0, 1999-05-01, 1999.

Moffitt, Robert A., "The Effect of Welfare on Marriage and Fertility: What Do We Know and What Do We Need to Know?" unpublished manuscript, December 1997.

Moffitt, Robert A., and LaDonna Pavetti, "Time Limits," Chicago, IL: Joint Center for Policy Research, Working Paper #91, May 1999.

Moffitt, Robert A., and David Stevens, *Changing Caseloads: Macro Influences and Micro Composition*, paper revised after presentation at "Welfare Reform Four Years Later: Progress and Prospects," Federal Reserve Bank of New York (November 17, 2000), December 2000.

118

Moffitt, Robert A., and M. Ver Ploeg (eds.), *Evaluating Welfare Reform: A Framework and Review of Current Work*, Washington, DC: National Academy Press, 1999.

Moulton, Brent R., "Random Group Effects and the Precision of Regression Estimates," *Journal of Econometrics*, 32L3850397, 1986.

Moynihan, Daniel Patrick, speech delivered to the U.S. Senate, Thursday August 1, 1996, reprinted as "When Principle Is At Issue," the *Washington Post*, August 4, 1996, p. C07.

Nathan, Richard P., and Thomas L. Gais, "Implementing the Personal Responsibility Act of 1996: A First Look," Federalism Research Group, The Nelson A. Rockefeller Institute of Government, State University of New York, May 2000, at http://rockinst.org/publications/federalism/first_look/index.html.

"Need Reprieve in Work Plan," *Los Angeles Times*, October 5, 1999, p. B-8.

Osborne, David, and Ted Gaebler, *Reinventing Government*, Reading, MA: Addison & Wesley, 1992.

Osborne, David, and Peter Plastrik, *Banishing Bureaucracy: The Five Strategies for Reinventing Government*, New York: Penguin USA, May 1998.

Overby, Russell, *Summary of Surveys of Welfare Recipients Employed or Sanctioned for Noncompliance*, Memphis, TN: University of Memphis, 1998.

Parrott, S., *Welfare Recipients Who Find Jobs: What Do We Know About Their Employment and Earnings?* Washington, D.C.: Center on Budget and Policy Priorities, 1998.

Pavetti, LaDonna, Nancy Wemmerus, and Amy Johnson, *Implementation of Welfare Reform in Virginia: A Work in Progress*, Washington, D.C.: Mathematica Policy Research, Inc., 1999.

Powers, Elizabeth T., "Block Granting Welfare: Fiscal Impact on the States," Washington, D.C.: The Urban Institute, Occasional Paper Number 23, 1999.

Primus, Wendell, Lynette Rawlings, Kathy Larin, and Kathryn Porter, *The Initial Impacts of Welfare Reform on the Incomes of Single-Mother Families*, Washington, D.C.: Center on Budget and Policy Priorities, 1999.

Rangarajan, Anu, *Keeping Welfare Recipients Employed: A Guide for States Designing Job Retention Services*, Princeton, N.J.: Mathematica Policy Research, Inc., June 1998.

Rangaranjan, Anu, and Tim Novak, "The Struggle to Sustain Employment: The Effectiveness of the Postemployment Services Demonstration," Princeton, N.J.: Mathematica Policy Research, Inc., MPR Reference No.: 8194-620, April 1999, at http://www.mathematica-mpr.com/strug-rpt.pdf.

Rector, Robert E., and Sarah E. Youssef, *The Determinants of Welfare Caseload Decline*, Washington, D.C.: The Heritage Foundation, 1999.

Riccio, James, and Daniel Friedlander, *GAIN: Program Strategies, Participation Patterns, and First-Year Impacts in Six Counties,* New York: Manpower Demonstration Research Corporation, 1992.

Riccio, James, Daniel Friedlander, and Stephen Freedman, *GAIN: Benefits, Costs, and Three-Year Impacts of a Welfare-to-Work Program.* New York: Manpower Demonstration Research Corporation, September 1994, at http://www.mdrc. org/Reports/GAINExSum/GAIN-ExSummary.htm.

Rivera, Carla, "Recipients Get Job Reprieve," *Los Angeles Times*, October 4, 1999, p. B-1.

Rivera, Carla, "Welfare Applicants to Receive Visits at Home," *Los Angeles Times*, September 17, 1999, B-1.

Roderick, Kevin, "State Officials Castigate L.A. County Over GAIN Project," *Los Angeles Times*, October 8, 1998, p. 1.

Saillant, Catherine, "Despite Deadline, Welfare Checks Continue," *Los Angeles Times*, Ventura County Edition, September 9, 1999, p. B-1.

Saillant, Catherine, "Healthy Economy Leaves Surplus for Welfare," *Los Angeles Times*, Ventura County Edition, April 20, 1999, p. B-1.

Schoeni, Robert F., and Rebecca M. Blank, "What Has Welfare Reform Accomplished? Impacts on Welfare Participation, Employment, Income, Poverty, and Family Structure," Santa Monica, CA: RAND, Labor & Population Working Paper Series 00-02, 2000.

Shuit, Douglas P., "Budget Cuts Threaten to Undermine GAIN Welfare: The State's Ambitious Education and Training Program Is Designed to End Dependency by Teaching Job Skills. A Battle Is Shaping Up to Keep the Money Flowing," *Los Angeles Times,* March 20, 1990, p. 3.

Smith, Steven Rathgeb, and Michael Lipsky, *Nonprofits for Hire: The Welfare State in the Age of Contracting*, Cambridge, MA: Harvard University Press: March 1993.

Speiglman, Richard, Lynn Fujiwara, Jean Norris, and Rex Green, *Alameda County CalWORKs Needs Assessment: A Look at Potential Health-Related Barriers to Self-Sufficiency*, Public Health Institute, August 30, 1999.

"State Deserves Welfare Break," *Los Angeles Times*, January 28, 1999, p. B-8.

State of California Economic Development Department, *Report on the Welfare to Work Grant Program Calendar Year 1998*, A Report to the California Legislature, Sacramento, CA, 1998.

State Policy Documentation Project (SPDP), *Separate State Programs and State-Only TANF Funds*, June 2000, at http://www.spdp.org/tanf/ssp_and_stateonly. pdf.

"States Get Welfare Reform Bonuses," *Los Angeles Times*, December 5, 1999, p. A-27.

Statewide Automated Welfare System Project: Multiple County Consortium Strategy, California Health and Welfare Agency Data Center, Report to the Legislature, November 1, 1995.

"TANF: Educating Clients About Sanctions," DHHS 0I6, OEI-09-98-00291, October 1999.

"TANF: Improving Client Sanction Notices," DHHS 0I6, OEI-09-98-00292, October 1999.

"TANF: Improving the Effectiveness of and Efficiency of Client Sanctions," DHHS-0I6, OEI-09-98-00290, July 1999.

"Target Welfare Fraud," *Los Angeles Times*, July 6, 1999, p. B-7.

"U.S. Approves Private Pact for Workfare," *Los Angeles Times*, January 21, 1989, p. 4.

U.S. Bureau of the Census, *Poverty in the United States: 1992*, Current Population Reports, Washington, D.C., September 1993.;

U.S. Committee on Ways and Means, *2000 Green Book: Background Material and Data on Programs Within the Jurisdiction of the Committee on Ways and Means*, "Section 13: Tax Provisions Related to Retirement, Health, Poverty, Employment, Disability and Other Social Issues," Washington, D.C.: U.S. Government Printing Office, October 6, 2000, pp. 808-811, at http://frwebgate. access.gpo.gov/cgi-bin/useftp.cgi?IPaddress=162.140.64.31&filename= wm014_13.pdf&directory=/diskb/wais/data/106_green_book.

U.S. Department of Health and Human Services, Administration for Children and Families, "State Welfare Demonstrations," Washington, D.C., October 7, 1996, at http://www.hhs.gov/news/press/1996pres/961007b.html.

U.S. Department of Health and Human Services, Administration for Children and Families, Office of the Assistant Secretary for Planning and Evaluation, *Setting the Baseline: A Report on State Welfare Waivers*, Washington, D.C., June 1997b , at http://aspe.os.dhhs.gov/hsp/fsp/waiver2/title.htm (accessed 1998).

U.S. Department of Health and Human Services, Office of Inspector General, *Temporary Assistance for Needy Families: Educating Clients About Sanctions*, Washington, D.C., 1999.

U.S. Department of Health and Human Services, Office of the Assistant Secretary for Planning, *Leavers' and Diversion Studies: Summary of Research on Welfare Outcomes Funded by ASPE*, Washington, D.C., June 2000, at http://aspe.os. dhhs.gov/hsp/leavers99.

U.S. Department of Labor, *History of Changes to the FLSA*, Washington, D.C., at http://www.dol.gov/dol/esa/public/minwage/coverage.htm.

U.S. Department of Labor, *Statement of the President on the Signing of the Small Business Job Protection Act of 1996*, August 20, 1996, Washington, D.C., at http://www.dol.gov/dol/esa/public/minwage/signing.htm.

U.S. Department of Labor, *Value of the Federal Minimum Wage, 1938–1997*, Washington, D.C., at http://www.dol.gov/dol/esa/public/minwage/chart2.htm.

U.S. General Accounting Office, *Welfare Reform: Early Fiscal Effects of the TANF Block Grant*, Report to the Chairman, Subcommittee on Human Resources, Committee on Ways and Means, House of Representatives, Washington, D.C., AIMD-98-137, August 18, 1998, at http://www.access.gpo.gov/cgi-bin/getdoc.cgi?dbname=gao&docid=f:ai98137.txt.pdf.

U.S. General Accounting Office, *Welfare Reform: Few States Are Likely to Use Simplified Food Stamp Program*, Washington, D.C., RCED 99-43, January 29, 1999, at http://www.gao.gov/.

U.S. General Accounting Office, *Welfare Reform: States Are Restructuring Programs to Reduce Welfare Dependence*, GAO/HEHS-98-109, Washington, D.C., June 1998.

U.S. General Accounting Office, *Welfare Reform: State Sanctions Policies and Number of Families Affected*, Washington, D.C., 2000.

U.S. General Accounting Office, *Welfare Reform: Transportation's Role in Moving from Welfare to Work*, Washington, D.C., May 1998.

Wallace, Geoffrey, and Rebecca M. Blank, "What Goes Up Must Come Down: Explaining Recent Changes in Public Assistance Caseloads," in Sheldon Danziger (ed.), *Economic Conditions and Welfare Reform*, Kalamazoo, MI: W.E. Upjohn Institute for Employment Research, 1999.

Waller, Maray, and Mark Allan Hughes, *Working Far From Home: Transportation and Welfare Reform in the Ten Big States*, Washington, D.C.: Progressive Policy Institute, August 1999.

Weisner, Constance, and Laura Schmidt, "Alcohol and Drug Problems among Diverse Health and Social Services Populations," *American Journal of Public Health*, Vol. 83, No. 6, June 1993.

Weissman, Evan, *Changing to a Work First Strategy: Lessons from Los Angeles County's GAIN Program for Welfare Recipients*, New York: Manpower Demonstration Research Corporation, 1997.

"Welfare Fraud Prevention and Investigative Functions of the Department of Social Services," at http://grandjury.co.la.ca.us/gjury99/mrbl.html; http://grandjury.co.la.ca.us/gjury99/REPORtgj-15.htm#Anchor-recommendations-63419.

Wiseman, Michael, "A Management Information Model for New-Style Public Assistance," Washington, D.C.: Urban Institute, Discussion Paper 99-10, August 1999, at http://newfederalism.urban.org/html/discussion99-10.html.

Wood, Tracy, "Private Approach to Public Welfare: An L.A. Innovation," *Los Angeles Times*, October 20, 1988, p. 1.

Wood, Tracy, "State Accepts Proposal for Private Firm's Role in Workfare Program," *Los Angeles Times*, October 25, 1998, p. 1.

Woodward, Albert, Joan Epstein, Joseph Gfroerer, Danile Melnick, Richard Thoreson, and Douglas Willson, "The Drug Abuse Treatment Gap: Recent Estimates," *Health Care Financing Review*, Vol. 18, No. 3, Spring 1997.

Zellman, Gail L., and A. Johansen, "Military Child Care: Toward an Integrated Delivery System," *Armed Forces & Society*, Vol. 21, No. 4, 1995, pp. 639–659.

Zellman, Gail L., Jacob A. Klerman, Elaine Reardon, Donna S. Farley, Nicole Humphrey, Tammi Chun, and Paul Steinberg, *Welfare Reform in California: State and County Implementation of CalWORKs in the First Year*, Santa Monica, CA: RAND, MR-1051-CDSS, 1999a.

Zellman, Gail L., Jacob A. Klerman, Elaine Reardon, and Paul Steinberg, *Welfare Reform in California: State and County Implementation of CalWORKs in the First Year—Executive Summary*, Santa Monica, CA: RAND, MR-1051/1-CDSS, 1999b.

Ziliak, James, David Figlio, Elizabeth Davis, and Laura Connolly, "Accounting for the Decline in AFDC Caseloads: Welfare Reform or Economic Growth?" Madison, WI: Institute for Research on Poverty Discussion Paper No. 1151-97, 1997.